The GOLF
HANDBOOK

The GOLF HANDBOOK

RICHARD BRADBEER
& IAN MORRISON

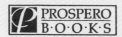

PROSPERO
B·O·O·K·S

Updated and reprinted 1998
Reprinted 1999

This edition produced for Prospero Books
A division of Chapters Inc.

First published in 1997 by Abbeydale Press
an imprint of Bookmart Limited
Desford Road, Enderby
Leicester LE9 5AD
England

Originally published in 1993 by Bookmart Limited
as *The Ultimate Golfer.*

ISBN 1-86147-006-1

Printed and bound in Singapore

*Page 1: Tiger Woods, 18th hole at St Andrews
Previous page: Jose-Maria Olazabal*

ACKNOWLEDGEMENTS

The publishers would like to thank:
Phil Sheldon Golf Picture Library, Barnet Herts EN5 2JQ (Tel 0181 440 1986/Fax 0181 440 9348)
for the pictures appearing on pages 1, 2, 19, 37, 43, 48, 49, 65, 80, 84, 91, 114, 115, 135, 155, 174, 199, 200,
206, 210, 211, 216, 220–1, 223, 226, 232.

Michael Hobbs Golf Collection for the pictures appearing on pages 5, 6–8, 17, 18, 28–30, 123, 135, 147, 152,
156, 164–70, 171–3, 175–6, 179–98, 201–5, 208–19, 222–56.

Sarah Fabian Baddiel, Golfiana, The Golf Gallery, London W1 (Tel. 0181 452 7243)
for the pictures appearing on pages 170, 177, 178, 215, 218, 237

Peter Dazeley for the pictures appearing on pages 38, 53, 103, 204, 205

PUBLISHER'S NOTE

The instructions in the book assume that the player is right-handed. If you are a left- handed
player you should reverse the instructions.

CONTENTS

Nick Faldo

THE WORLD OF CHAMPIONSHIP GOLF

PLAYING THE
GAME

INTRODUCTION

One of the truly great things about the game of golf is that it can be played by men and women of all ages and walks of life. It is a game that requires concentration with both the body and the mind, but the rewards are so great that it makes all of the effort worthwhile.

EQUIPMENT

CLUBS

Golf clubs can now be purchased at many outlets, but it is always best to deal with one that is qualified to give you the correct advice. Value for money does not always mean buying the cheapest clubs. If you deal with known brands, you will be able to get a comprehensive back-up service.

CLUBS

Top: The current trend is for clubheads with a cavity back. Bottom: A blade-type clubhead.

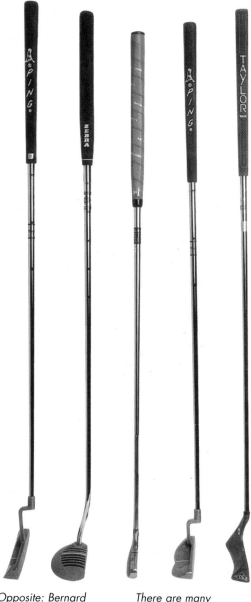

Opposite: Bernard Langer

Previous page: Cherry Hills

There are many different shapes of putter heads; here are several of the most popular.

A HALF-SET FOR BEGINNERS
When you first start playing golf
it is not necessary to buy fourteen
clubs, seven is sufficient for any
new player. A good
combination to have
would be a 3-wood, 3-,
5-, 7-, 9-irons, a sand
wedge and a putter. When
buying your first set of clubs
it is best to seek the advice
of a PGA Professional.

SHAFTS
There are a few points to bear in
mind when you purchase new or
second-hand clubs. The most
flexible shafts 'L' are generally
used for ladies' golf clubs. 'R'
are used by the majority of
men and 'S' by stronger
players. Always check that
the shaft is correct for your
requirements.

*A half-set of clubs suitable
for a beginner comprising
a 3-wood, 3-, 5-, 7-, and
9-irons a sand wedge
and a putter.*

*Two hand-made
wooden golf clubs.*

GRIP

Check that the grip is the right thickness for your hands and that all the clubs in the set have the same grip. To help control the hold on the club most people wear a thin leather glove on their top hand. Shaft flexibility and the size of the grip can affect the swing weight and the overall weight of the club. Always try the clubs before you make a purchase.

SWING WEIGHTING

Swing weighting is a method of producing a set of clubs that feels the same when each club is swung. The swing weight of a club is related to the flex in the shaft. The ladies' shaft (L) is fitted to clubs with a swing weight C6 to C8, the men's regular shaft (R) is between C9 and D2, and the men's stiff shaft (S) is between D3 and D6.

From left to right: a no. 1-wood with graphite shaft and head; a metal-headed no. 1-wood with a steel shaft - note the head is larger and designed to give more power; the last three are a set of 1, 3 and 5 wooden clubs with steel shafts.

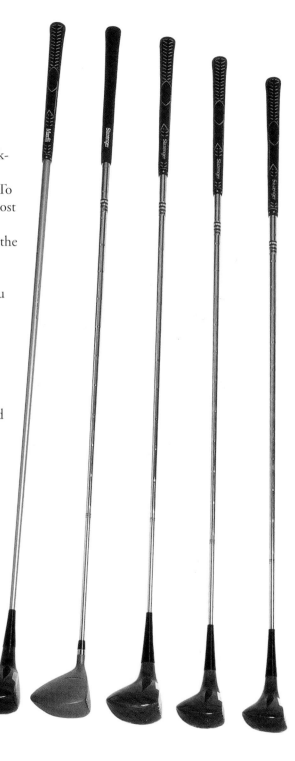

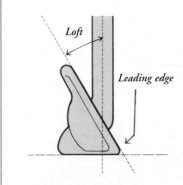

Loft

Leading edge

LOFT AND DISTANCE

This shows that the loft on the clubface is the number of degrees that the clubface is set back from a vertical line running through the centre of the shaft of the club. To make sure you aim correctly you must always position the leading edge of the club at 90 degrees to the ball-to-target line.

IRONS	LOFT	LENGTH OF SHAFT In (mm)	APPROX DISTANCE Yd(ms)
2	18°	38½ (978)	190 (174)
3	22°	38 (965)	180 (165)
4	26°	37½ (953)	170 (155)
5	30°	37 (940)	160 (146)
6	34°	36½ (927)	150 (137)
7	38°	36 (914)	140 (128)
8	42°	35½ (902)	130 (119)
9	46°	35 (889)	120 (110)
Pitching wedge	52°	35 (889)	100 (91)
Sand wedge	58°	35 (889)	80 (73)
Woods			
1	12°	43 (1092)	240 (219)
2	16°	42½ (1080)	220 (201)
3	20°	42 (1066)	200 (183)
4	24°	41½ (1054)	180 (165)
5	28°	41 (1040	170 (155)

LOFT AND DISTANCE

You are allowed to have fourteen clubs in your bag when playing golf. Each club serves a different purpose and is used for hitting different distances. As the number of each club increases the loft goes up 4 degrees, and the length of the shaft decreases by ½ inch (12.5mm). The longest club has less loft, it can therefore hit the ball further. The head on the irons gets larger with a deeper face as the irons get shorter. This enables the club to hit the ball up in the air.

A set of clubs consisting of three metal-headed woods (nos. 1, 3 and 5), and nine irons (nos. 3 to 9, a wedge and a sand wedge). With the addition of a putter and either another wood or iron they would make up the club set.

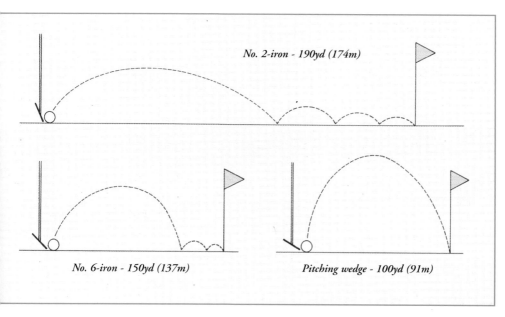

No. 2-iron - 190yd (174m)

No. 6-iron - 150yd (137m)

Pitching wedge - 100yd (91m)

THE GOLF BALL

Golf balls used all over the world
are now of universal size - 1.68in
(42.5mm) in diameter and
weighing 1.62oz (46g). There
are basically three types of balls
on the market, each varying in
the materials used and in their
performance and durability.

BALATA
Balata is the first choice of low
handicap and professional players,
who demand maximum feel and
spin for control at all times. This
ball is made up of a liquid centre,
elastic winding and a Balata cover.

*A ball being
wound.*

*Many golf balls
today have club
or company
logos put on
them. Here the
balls are being
checked before
the logo is
stamped on.*

THREE-PIECE BALL

The three piece ball still gives the feel that professionals are looking for, but it has a different cover making it more durable. The centre of the ball is a rubber-type material which is then wound round with rubber thread. The third part of this type of ball is the cover which in many cases is made of surlyn.

A two-piece ball

The three-piece ball, starting as a pellet which is rounded and then smoothed and wound round with the rubber thread. The cover is compressed together and the dimple formation pressed on.

TWO-PIECE BALL

The two piece ball is probably the most popular ball, giving both distance and durability. It is made up of a solid centre and a man-made cover. Because of its hardness this type of ball, whilst travelling further is often difficult to pitch and putt with. The dimple pattern on the golf ball varies from one to another; each manufacturer will of course state that theirs is the best!

Balls being painted

A two-piece ball. The centre of the ball is rounded and then the granules shown here are made into the cover.

OTHER EQUIPMENT
Tee pegs are either wooden or plastic. It is largely a matter of personal preference which type you choose. One of the other items that you will find useful is a ball marker.

SHOES
The range of golfing shoes on the market today is enormous. The main choice to be made is whether to buy spiked or non-spiked shoes. Spikes will give you a better grip, but they are heavier and not necessary on the lighter parts of the course. If you do wear spikes be careful not to damage the greens.

A pair of spiked golf shoes.

Golf clubs are still made by hand.

PLAYING IN COLD WEATHER
Several layers of clothing will restrict your swing, so it is advisable to select lightweight thermal clothing and a waterproof jacket. Large mittens are an excellent way of keeping your hands warm. If your hands get cold you will lose control of the club. Always keep your head covered.

PLAYING IN THE RAIN

It is important to select a light-weight waterproof jacket that will not restrict your swing. Umbrellas are also useful for protecting yourself and your equipment from the elements between shots. One of the greatest hazards of playing in the rain is that if the grip becomes sodden it is extremely difficult to keep a firm hold on the club. A clean towel is useful for drying the grip and you can wear all-weather gloves which will enable you to keep a firmer hold. Remember that rain gathers on the golf ball which will affect the flight of the ball. Consider using a more lofted club than you would usually, for example, a 5-wood instead of a 3-wood. This will help the ball to become airborne more quickly. If due to incessant rain your feet sink into the turf at the address your feet will become lower than the level of the ball. To compensate for this move your hands down the grip slightly. If the ground is slippery make sure your shoes are full studded.

Bernard Langer well wrapped up against the elements.

Opposite: Ernie Els.

STARTING OUT

One of the things that you hear so often on the golf course is people saying 'Yes, I play golf, but I am so inconsistent'. Golf is a game that is very much in the mind, and you have to work hard at understanding and mastering the basic requirements for consistent and improving play. Everybody wants results, and results come from a sound routine and knowledge of technique, but they also come from confidence.

AIMING THE CLUB

To ensure that you hit the ball in the right direction you must first be able to imagine the shot you are going to play. Establish the 'ball-to-target line'. If the target is far away select a point closer to you and in line with the ball and target. Always double-check your aim. The part of the club which directs the ball is the leading edge. This must be positioned square to the ball-to-target line and at right angles to your shoulders. If the leading edge of the clubface is turned either to the left (a closed face), or out to the right (an open face), this will send the ball off course.

THE CLUBHEAD

The toe of the club.

The heel of the club; with an iron this is called the socket.

The face. This is the part of the club with which you usually strike the ball. The ball should be lined up with the centre of the clubface.

POSITION OF THE BALL

The no.1- wood is correctly positioned to the ball. The ball should be teed-up so that half of the ball is visible above the clubface.

The leading edge. Each clubhead is different in shape and loft but they all have a leading edge.

LIE OF THE CLUB

The lie of the club is too flat, the heel is lifted off the ground.

A

The lie of this club is too upright, the toe is lifted off the ground.

B

This is the correct lie. There should be a slight gap between the toe of the club and the ground.

C

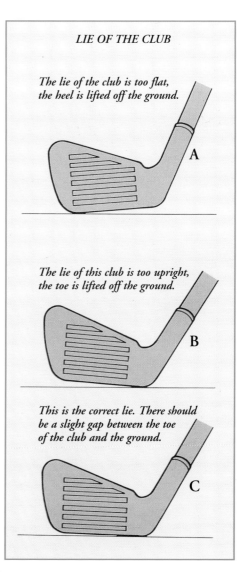

OPEN AND CLOSED CLUBFACES

The tees indicate the 'ball-to-target line'. Here the 3-wood is set square.

The leading edge is turned to the left, closing the clubface.

The leading edge is square to the ball-to-target line.

The toe of the club is turned in, closing the clubface.

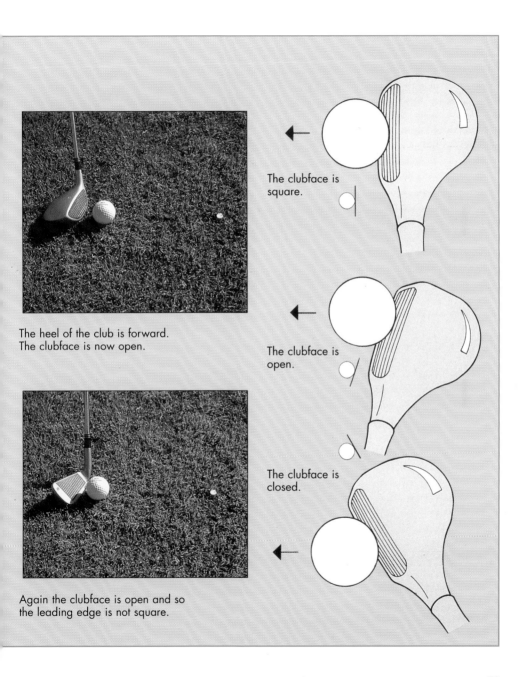

The heel of the club is forward.
The clubface is now open.

The clubface is square.

The clubface is open.

The clubface is closed.

Again the clubface is open and so
the leading edge is not square.

BALL-TO-TARGET LINE

1 Standing behind the ball will help you to establish the ball-to-target line.

2 The clubhead is set on the chosen ball-to-target line.

3 Always double-check your aim by looking at the target.

Key Points Card	
	Remarks
1	Always aim with the leading edge of the golf club.
2	Stand behind the ball looking at the target.
3	Select a point closer to you on the ball-to-target line.
4	Place the clubhead so the ball is in line with the centre of the clubface.

THE GRIP (HOLD)

Hold the club the way that feels most comfortable to you. Start by learning the correct hold for the left hand. Do not alter the position of your left hand when you place your right hand on the club. The two hands must be trained together, as one unit.

THE LEFT HAND

1 Part of the grip should be outside your left hand. This is more comfortable than holding the end of the grip and will help to give more control.

2 The grip of the club should lie diagonally across the palm of your hand approximately ¼ in (6mm) from the base of your little finger and across to the middle joint of your forefinger.

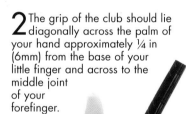

3 When the hand is closed you should be able to see at least two knuckles of your left hand.

4 The left thumb needs to be just to the right of the centre of the grip. This will form a V-shape with your forefinger which will point between your face and your shoulder.

THE RIGHT HAND

1 When you place your right hand on the grip do not move your left hand. The palm of the right hand faces the target. The grip should lie in the middle joints of the first three fingers.

2 The left thumb will now fit inside the right hand. The right thumb should lie just to the left of the centre of the grip, so forming a V-shape.

3 Both 'V's must point between your face and right shoulder.

TYPES OF GRIP (HOLD)

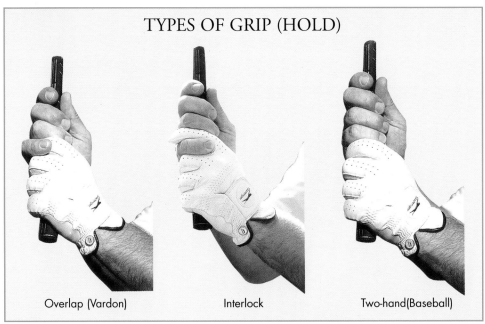

Overlap (Vardon)   Interlock   Two-hand(Baseball)

THE PROFESSIONALS

Harry Vardon, c. 1905. The overlapping grip is otherwise known as the Vardon grip because Vardon was one of the first great players to use it. This is the most popular of the three grips.

GRIP PRESSURE

1 It is important to maintain the correct pressure on the grip. At the top of the backswing you need to feel you are holding the club with the last three fingers of your left hand. This gives you control and at the same time enables wrist movement. In your right hand feel the pressure in your middle two fingers.

2 The hands should always be close together to enable them to work as a single unit.

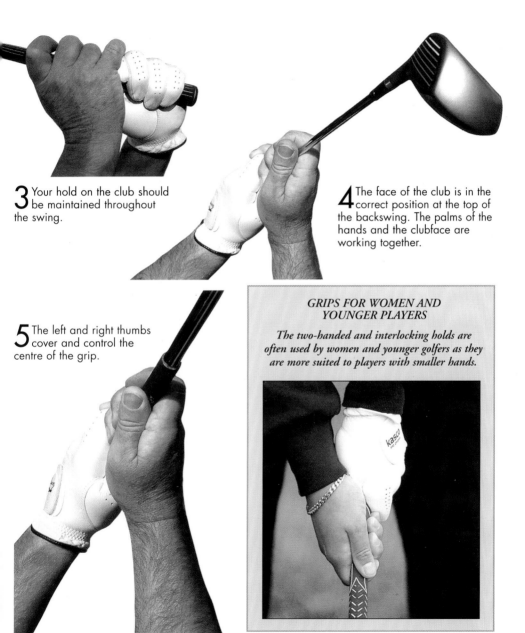

3 Your hold on the club should be maintained throughout the swing.

4 The face of the club is in the correct position at the top of the backswing. The palms of the hands and the clubface are working together.

5 The left and right thumbs cover and control the centre of the grip.

GRIPS FOR WOMEN AND YOUNGER PLAYERS

The two-handed and interlocking holds are often used by women and younger golfers as they are more suited to players with smaller hands.

29

THE PROFESSIONALS

Arnold Palmer of the USA using the overlapping hold on the club. See how his hands are held high. This was a feature of the great man's play.

COMMON FAULTS

You will often find you are having problems because you are using the wrong grip. Watch out for the faults shown below and always check you have the right grip.

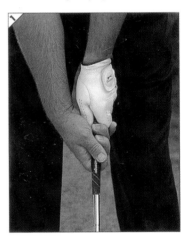

Key Points Card	
	Remarks
1	Once you have the correct left-hand grip, do not alter it when you place your right hand on the club.
2	Remember the position of the thumbs helps to control the position of the clubface at the top of the backswing.
3	Maintain the correct grip pressure. You must not let go of the club during the shot.

STRONG GRIP

1 The 'V's are pointing to the right of the right shoulder. This closes the clubface.

2 The face of the club is pointing to the sky, which can result in hooking left.

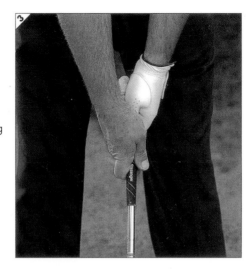

WEAK GRIP

3 & 4 the hands are pointing towards the left shoulder. This will increase the loft on the clubface during the backswing and the ball will probably be sliced to the right.

5 The left thumb is extended down the grip of the club. The danger is that it will be difficult to place the right hand correctly on the club, causing a loss of hand control.

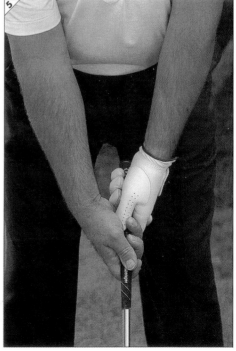

STANCE

Having established how to hold and aim the club it is now important to check your posture. Without the correct posture you will find it extremely hard to keep good balance and create the correct movements. Follow the steps shown and in particular note the angle of the spine. As a general rule your feet should be shoulder width apart when playing with woods and then moved closer together for shorter clubs.

1 Relax. Stand with your arms at your sides and feet shoulder width apart.

2 Bend forward from the hips. Your hips should go back and head and shoulders forward. Keep your back straight.

3 Maintaining the same spinal angle, let your arms hang down freely from your shoulders.

BODY ALIGNMENT

1 Shoulders, hips, knees and feet should be square, parallel to the ball.

BODY ALIGNMENT

To obtain the correct alignment to the target imagine a railway line - the clubhead, ball and target are on one rail and your feet, knees, hips and shoulders on the other. This will help you ensure that you are standing parallel to the target. This is called a square set-up.

2 Holding the club, flex your legs slightly, and let your hands hang down comfortably. Your right forearm will be slightly lower than your left arm.

POSTURE

To help yourself adopt the correct posture follow the routine shown below for every shot you play.

1 Stand upright, check that you have a square set-up parallel to the ball-to-target line.

2 Keeping your back straight lean forward and flex your legs towards one another

POSTURE FROM BEHIND

3 The spine tilts to the right. This should occur naturally if the shoulders are square, with the left hand at the top of the grip.

4 The feet are wider apart now that a longer club is being used.

BALL POSITION

The position of the ball in relation to your feet will vary according to the length of the club. With longer clubs the ball is further forward in the stance (just inside the left heel). As the club gets shorter move the ball back towards the middle of the stance. The ball is also positioned further away from the player when longer clubs are used.

MEDIUM SHOTS

3 For the medium clubs the ball has moved further back. Its position is more central.

LONG SHOTS

2 Position the ball so it forms a right angle from just inside your left foot to the ball-to-target line. Feet shoulder width apart.

1 The body is square to the ball-to-target line.

4 As the club gets shorter move your feet closer together. Head still behind the ball.

SUMMARY

In the following three pictures the same grip - the overlap - is being used for each type of club. In each case the club is extended from the left arm and the left hand is in line with the inside of the left leg. You can see clearly that both 'V's are pointing between the face and right shoulder.

As the club gets shorter then the ball is positioned further back in the stance and the feet move closer together.

LONG SHOTS

1 Ball inside the left foot, feet shoulder width apart, head behind the ball and weight evenly distributed.

MEDIUM SHOTS

2 Ball central in the stance, feet slightly closer together and arms hanging down comfortably.

EXERCISE

This exercise without a club shows the correct hand, arm and body movements for the takeaway. You need the correct posture to do this. Follow through to a point about waist high.

SHORT SHOTS

3 Ball further back in the stance and closer to the player, and slightly more weight on the left leg.

Key Points Card	
	Remarks
	Without the correct posture it is hard to swing correctly.
2	Timing, rhythm and balance are the key to a good swing.
3	Aim, grip, posture, body alignment and ball position have to be correct.

THE PROFESSIONALS

Jose-Maria Olazabal of Spain is seen checking his aim before playing a 1-iron. He is using the overlapping (Vardon) grip.

THE SWING

Having mastered the routine for making a good sound address position you are ready to attempt the movements required for the best possible golf swing. The following four series of pictures show the movements for the long (full), medium and short swing. Remember to check your aim, grip and stance before you start to swing.

THE PROFESSIONALS

Laura Davies demonstrates a complete follow-through which is a feature of a good swing.

THE FULL SWING

1 Position the ball level with the inside of the left foot. Stand with a relaxed posture and alignment.

4 Transfer body-weight on to your left side. Release the clubhead to the target with your arms together.

2 The takeaway should be a single movement, with your wrists not cocking before waist height.

3 At the top of the backswing, make a full shoulder turn. The club shaft should be parallel to the target line.

5 Bend your right leg at the knee. Turn your shoulders through allowing your head to look at the result.

6 At this point your hands should be high and your arms together and well balanced. Maintain the grip.

THE MEDIUM SWING

Position the ball centrally in your stance and stand with your arms hanging down comfortably.

Your body should move together but do not cock your wrists until waist height.

Keep your head steady. Do not take the club as far back in the medium swing as in the full swing.

THE SHORT SWING

Note the position of the arms and wrists. You cock your wrists much earlier for the short swing.

Take the club up much more quickly with less left foot and body movement.

Don't take your hands much higher than your shoulders. Note the hand and wrist position.

As you start the downswing, your legs and arms should work together, transfer weight on to your left leg.

Your head is brought through the swing by your right shoulder.

The movement in body-weight should take the left shoe over slightly.

Keep your wrists cocked as you start the downswing.

Head steady at impact.

Balanced follow-through with your arms together.

WOMEN'S SWING

Even though women have a different
physique from men, the same principles
of the golf swing apply. However, a good
posture is particularly essential to enable
the female player to make a good
shoulder turn, both on the backswing
and follow-through, as well as a good
free arm movement.

1 Stand with a good posture, your arms hanging down, body aligned square and legs flexed at the knee.

2 A good one-piece takeaway, with the hands and the clubhead working together.

3 Fold your right arm with your elbow pointing down to the ground.

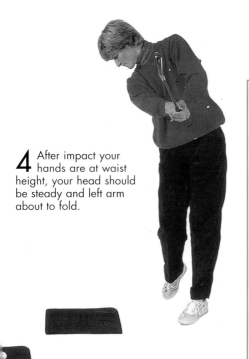

4 After impact your hands are at waist height, your head should be steady and left arm about to fold.

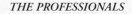

THE PROFESSIONALS

Alison Nicholas of England is seen here clearing the lower half of the body through impact so that the arms and club can be swung towards the target.

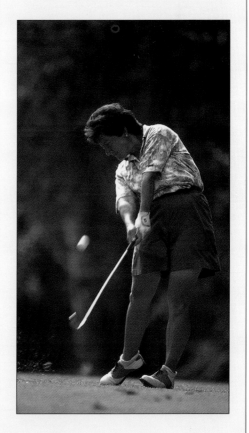

5 At the end of your follow-through your body should be facing the target and hands high.

GRIP AND BALL ALIGNMENT

The address position is a rehearsal for the impact the clubhead is going to make with the ball. Your hand position in relation to the golf ball is very important.

HANDS TOO FAR FORWARD

2 Both hands and the grip of the club are in front of the ball. Looking down the club both hands will be to the left causing an early wrist cock.

HANDS TOO FAR BACK

1 Both hands and the grip of the club are behind the ball. Looking down the club both hands will be to the right causing the hand action on the take-away to be too late.

CORRECT POSITION

3 The left hand just covers the inside of the left leg and is in line with the left side of the ball. The palm of the right hand and the leading edge of the golf club are aligned with the back of the ball.

RIGHT HAND

1 The palm of the hand should be in line with the back of the ball and facing the ball-to-target line.

2 The position of the hand relative to the ball when holding the grip of the club.

LEFT HAND

3 The back of the left hand should be facing the target and hanging over the left side of the ball.

THE GRIP

5 The back of the left hand should be facing the target and hanging over the left side of the ball.

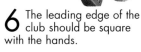

4 The left hand closed illustrating where it should be in relation to the ball at impact.

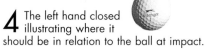

6 The leading edge of the club should be square with the hands.

45

TAKEAWAY AND BACKSWING

The takeaway is the beginning of the backswing. This must be a one-piece movement, with the left and right sides moving together. Your elbows must remain the same distance apart as they were at the address, and you must keep the head of the club square with your shoulders.

Note the difference in angle that occurs between long and short clubs.

3 The completed backswing for all long clubs. The shoulders have turned 90 degrees and the hips 45 degrees. The left arm is comfortably straight and the right arm bent with the elbow pointing to the ground just behind the right foot.

NO.1-WOOD

1 From the address position, as the club and arms travel beyond the right side, body-weight is transferred on to the instep of the right foot. The left hand, the back of which was pointing towards the target, will now face away from you.

2 The arms move together and stay the same distance apart as they were at the address. The clubhead, shaft, and grip are parallel with the ball-to-target line.

SHORT IRON

1 The wrists cock sooner at the start of the backswing with the short iron. The hands and arms are used to make the action, rather than the body.

2 Again the left arm and the club on the ground are in line with one another. Because the ball is now closer to you the club will come up at a steeper angle. This in turn will give a steeper attack on the ball.

3 At the top of the swing the wrists are fully cocked at shoulder height. The head is steady and there is less body movement than with longer clubs.

4 From a different angle you can see how there is less body movement.

LONG AND
SHORT CLUBS

1 With the long clubs,
the arms and club move
without an early wrist action, whereas
with shorter clubs the wrists take the
club back.

2 The angle you swing the club
at alters with the distance
that you stand from the ball.

Key Points Card	
	Remarks
1	The takeaway is a one-piece movement.
2	Transfer your body weight smoothly on to the instep of your right foot.
3	Keep the clubhead square to your shoulders.
4	Keep your left arm straight.
5	Keep your head still, looking at the ball.

THE PROFESSIONALS

Davis Love III of America is seen here just after impact. His head is held steady and his right leg and foot are transferring weight on to the left side.

THE PROFESSIONALS

Greg Norman of Australia is one of the world's most exciting players. This picture shows the force with which he hits the ball, allowing the right shoulder and right side to keep moving through impact and his very individual foot action.

EXERCISE

Practise holding the shaft of the club further down. Work on the shoulder hip and leg movement at the start of the swing. See how when you cock the wrists the handle of the club breaks away from your arm.

THE DOWNSWING AND FOLLOW-THROUGH

The downswing is the path of the clubhead from the top of the backswing down to the ball on impact. The follow-through is the path of the club after impact. The club, wrists, arms body and legs must all work smoothly together so that the clubhead arrives square-on to the ball.

LONG CLUBS

1 The lower part of the body moves towards the target. This keeps the head steady and the right shoulder back at the start of the downswing, ensuring the shoulders will be square to the ball-to-target line at impact.

2 The whole of the right side continues to move through impact unrestricted by the head.

3 Hands high, body well-balanced and spinal angle maintained. This shot will finish just to the left of the centre of the fairway.

MEDIUM CLUBS

1 The legs and arms again pull the club down, with the head held steady.

Key Points Card	
	Remarks
1	The club, wrists, arms, body and legs must all work together.
2	Transfer your weight smoothly from right to left.
3	Hit through the ball, keeping your head down and body still.
4	Follow through until hips and body face the target.

2 The arms and shoulder swing the club through to the target.

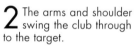

3 The body is facing the target with body-weight on the left side.

SHORT IRONS

1 Downward strike, again the shoulders are back ready to be square to the target at impact.

2 This is an unrestricted movement through the shot with the left side.

3 The water was no problem because the club had plenty of loft and did not stop on the shot.

LONG SHOT

The downswing has brought the weight of the body on to the left side; the shoulders are square to the target, and legs clear the hips to allow the hands and arms to extend and swing the clubhead to the target. The spinal angle is being maintained to enable the right shoulder to be lowered through impact rather than the left shoulder.

THE PROFESSIONALS

Fred Couples of the USA showing a well-balanced follow-through. The angle of the spine is maintained throughout the shot.

SHORT SHOT

The downswing movements through the legs and hips transfer weight on to the left side and keep the club low to the ground at, and after, impact.

SWING PATH

The ground between the player and the golf club is called 'the inside', and the ground on the other side is called 'the outside'. The correct swing path is from 'in to square', and 'in' again. This means that the clubhead is taken back on the inside, and after impact the follow-through should continue on the inside.

1 The ground between the player and the golf club is called 'the inside'.

3 And onwards to the top of the backswing.

4 The clubhead comes down to the ball on the inside. Then the hands release the clubhead to the ball.

2 On the takeaway, due to the body pivoting the club travels over the ground called the inside.

5 Through impact, the clubhead and shoulders are square to the ball-to-target line.

6 After impact the body continues to move through to face the target.

7 The arms are together and body-weight is on the outside of the left shoe.

8 Complete follow-through. The body has moved to face the target.

55

SWING PATH

The direction the clubhead is travelling in at impact will govern how the ball will start in its flight. In-to-out the ball will start right. Out-to-in the ball will start left. In-to-square and again the ball will fly straight.

In-to-out ◄ ◄ ◄ ◄ ◄ ◄ ◄ ◄

Out-to-in ◄ ◄ ◄ ◄ ◄ ◄ ◄ ◄

Ball-to-target line _____

FLIGHT PATH

If the ball swerves in its flight it is because it has side spin on it. The clubface should be square at impact. Hit with an open face the ball will swerve to the right and with a closed face to the left.

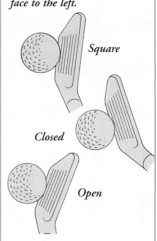

Square

Closed

Open

SWING PATH: EXAMPLE TWO

1 & 2 The club moving towards the target. The head is held steady, shoulders square, weight on the left leg, and right foot moving on to the instep, with the leg bending at the knee.

3 & 4 The clubhead is square to the shoulders with the toe of the club overtaking the heel and pointing to the sky. The left forearm and elbow are helping to keep the arms together. The head is still.

5 & 6 Body facing the target, hands under the club, right shoe up on to the toe and right shoulder still slightly lower than the left.

57

SWING PATH: EXAMPLE THREE

1 Address all set. Shoulders square. Arms are hanging down. Back straight and tilted over the ground. Head clear of chest.

2 Moving down on the inside. Hips clearing and shoulders ready to move squarely through impact.

3 Notice the divot is square with the line-up.

4 The follow-through is complete. The angle of spine is the same as for the address. The divot has gone to the left.

WARM-UP EXERCISES

ARMS AND HANDS

It is essential in the playing of all golf shots that you maintain your hold on the grip of the club. To enable you to do this from the start warm up before you play. This exercise will give you a stretching feeling in your arms and also rehearse the action of the arms for the back-swing. Feel the pressure of your hold on the club in the last three fingers of your left hand and practise maintaining it.

1 Stand in the address position.

2 Stand upright, lift the club up above your head and between your right shoulder and the right side of your head. Keep your arms the same distance apart at the elbows as they were in the address position.

3 Repeat this action for the left side.

59

SHOULDERS

These movements are designed to understand and practise the correct shoulder movements and angle of the spine.

1 Hold the golf club in front of you, across your chest. Assume the correct posture.

2 Keeping your head still, turn your shoulders so that the grip points outside your right shoe. The hips and legs respond to this shoulder turn. Turn around the spine position set at the address, as the spine gives the tilt to the shoulder turn.

3 From the backswing position, keeping your head still, transfer your weight with a leg and hip movement. Bring your shoulders down and around to complete a follow-through position. Note how this shoulder movement turns your head so that it is looking along the ball-to-target line.

HIPS

Both the shoulder and hip actions are
essential to give the arms and
hands the correct angle of attack
on the golf ball. Repeat these hip movements several times. The main point to
note here is that the hips turn on a line
parallel to the ground.

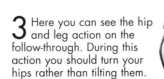

1 Hold the club so that the
shaft is parallel to the
ground, Set your body in
the correct posture for the
address position.

2 Keeping your head still, turn
your body with the golf club
parallel to the ground. This
practises the correct hip turn on
the backswing.

3 Here you can see the hip
and leg action on the
follow-through. During this
action you should turn your
hips rather than tilting them.

THE SWING

The golf swing is a series of movements, not least of all of the golf club itself. Although people say let the club do the work in fact the club can do very little on its own, and this final exercise will help you accelerate the movement of the club.

1 Hold any club quite far down the grip and roughly in the centre of the stance but with your right hand only.

2 Take the club back a short distance, note how the right arm bends at the elbow.

3 Now swing the club with your hand and arm across your shoulder line as fast as you can. Maintain your hold on the grip of the club. This should give you the feeling of releasing the clubhead. Repeat several times. Ensure you do not hit the ground.

5 Swing the club back a short distance with your left arm and hand, and then accelerate the club across your shoulder line as fast as you can while maintaining your hold on the grip. Again you do not want to hit the ground.

4 Next hold the grip of the club with your left hand. Position the club in the centre of your stance.

EXERCISE

Take any club: hold it the wrong way around. Make a full back and through swing as if hitting a ball. The shaft and grip will make a swishing sound. The noise should occur at and after the area of impact.

6 Again this should give you the feeling of releasing the club-head and shaft past your body.

63

STRETCHING

1 Taking two or three clubs with similar lengths of shafts, set up for the address position. Do not use a ball. Make sure that you can control how far the clubs go back on the backswing and the follow-through.

2 & 3 Make this full swing as shown here. The weight of the clubs will help stretch the arm and shoulder movement.

Opposite: Colin Montgomerie

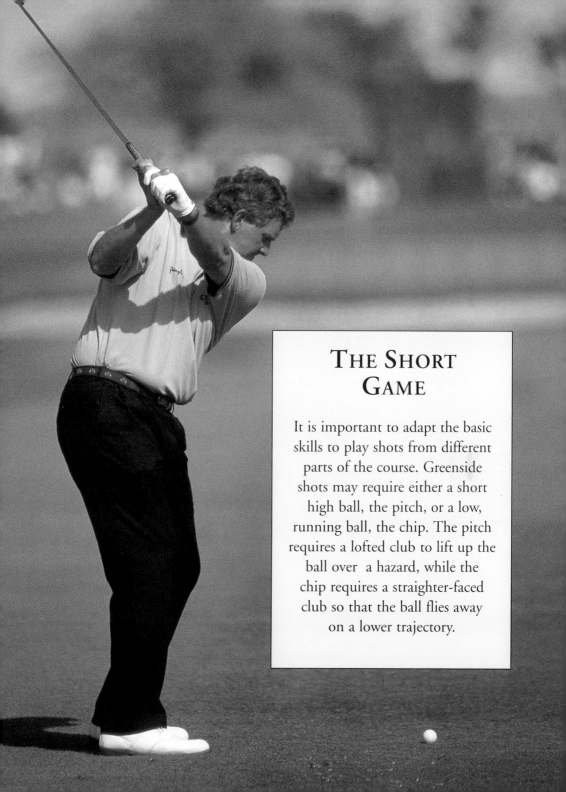

THE SHORT GAME

It is important to adapt the basic skills to play shots from different parts of the course. Greenside shots may require either a short high ball, the pitch, or a low, running ball, the chip. The pitch requires a lofted club to lift up the ball over a hazard, while the chip requires a straighter-faced club so that the ball flies away on a lower trajectory.

PITCHING

The pitch is used when you need the ball to fly high in the air over a hazard, such as a bunker or a bank. A lofted club - the sand or pitching wedge - is used to give the ball lift. Your choice of club will depend on the lie of the ball and the distance to the target. The pitching wedge is the more versatile of these two clubs because the sand wedge must only be used in a bunker or on a soft grassy lie.

2 With the bunkers in the way the ball must go in the air.

3 Use the full length of the club. The club and ball are lined up to the flag. The shoulders are square with the feet, legs and hips open.

1 Set the leading edge square. position the ball slightly off centre, closer to the heel of the club. Stand with the left foot back to give an open stance.

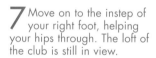

4 Turn your shoulders and legs slightly for the swing. Keep your head quite still and make sure your hands and clubface are in shape together.

5 This shot was a ball-and-turf contact caused by the shift in body-weight and the hands and arms hitting down and through at impact.

7 Move on to the instep of your right foot, helping your hips through. The loft of the club is still in view.

6 At impact shift your weight on to the left side, clearing the hips. With your shoulders still square, your arms and golf club send the ball to the flag.

8 Watch the result with the club pointing directly at the flag.

THE SHORT
PITCH

1 If the ball is lying in nice
soft grass use the sand
wedge. Maintain the same
grip as before but position
the ball slightly further back
in the stance. The left hand
is still in line with the inside
of the left leg.

2 Take the club back with an
early wrist cock, supporting
the movement with your shoulders. The whole of the face of
the club is visible.

3 At impact your left arm,
the shaft and head of the
club return in to line, as they
were at the address position.
Transfer your body-weight
over to the left side, to help
keep the clubhead low
through the shot.

4 The right side should
move under your head
and shoulders. It is the shape
of the clubhead that gives the
ball height and direction.

PITCHING

This is how the sole of the pitching wedge sits on the ground.

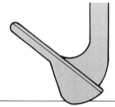

The leading edge of the sand wedge is off the ground. The back of the sole is rounded to give the bounce you need to move enough sand to get the ball out of the greenside bunker.

When attempting a pitch shot it is the loft on the clubface that lifts the ball into the air, not a lifting action made by the body and hands.

On the takeaway and backswing the body stays still as the wrists and arms take the club back up.

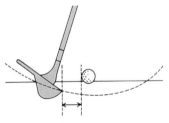

The distance between the ball and the club should be between 1½ and 2ins (35-50mm).

A SHORT HIGH LOB SHOT

1 Your legs should be more flexed at the knee. Position the ball quite close to your feet and not too far back in the stance.

3 Keeping your head steady, make a smooth transference of weight on to your left side. The clubhead should still be extended from the shoulders.

2 Just before impact keep your wrists cocked and pull the club down to the ball with your arms and body-weight.

4 Follow through with your right shoulder lower than your left. Your head should naturally turn to face the target.

5 Watch the result from a well-balanced position.

THE PITCHING WEDGE

The pitching wedge is a very versatile golf club which is used to play high shots to the green from many different distances.

On the following page the distance of the ball from the feet slightly increases as the length of the shot increases, and the arms and shoulders swing back further as the shot being played gets longer.

In each case the hands and arms are working together to create a square impact. The head is held steady and the weight of the lower body moves on to the left side, with shoulders becoming square to the ball at impact. The angle of the spine is maintained through impact.

Striking with the pitching or sand wedge is what is called a ball-to-turf-contact. This is achieved with the correct movements of the lower body-weight, and the arms and club on the downswing and through impact. It is very important that you do not let the club overtake your arms as you hit the ball. You must never try and lift the ball off the ground up into the air, use the loft on the clubface.

Changes in the swing as the player moves further back from the target. In each case the club is swung further back as the shot being played gets longer.

71

PITCHING WEDGE SHOTS FROM
DIFFERENT DISTANCES

In each of the four series of pictures the player is further away from the target. Notice how the distance that the club is swung back and the extent the body moves through the shot increase with the longer shots.

THE PROFESSIONALS

Nick Faldo of England playing a pitch up and over a bank to the green.
The clubface has still got loft on it. Notice how he is not wearing a glove
on his left hand. Many of the best players remove their glove for
pitching, chipping and putting.

CHIPPING

This is a low running ball, rather than a high ball. You can use your putter for this shot but often the fairway or the approach to the green is too wet, or not smooth enough, to roll the ball over. The ideal club loft for this shot is a 4-iron, but you can also use a 6- or a 7-iron.

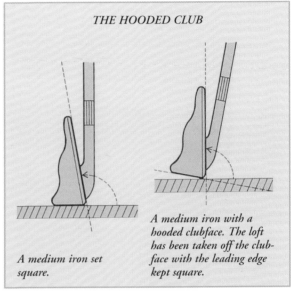

THE HOODED CLUB

A medium iron set square.

A medium iron with a hooded clubface. The loft has been taken off the clubface with the leading edge kept square.

1 Your hands should be a little ahead of the ball , this has the effect of taking loft from the face of the club, so that the clubface is not closed but hooded. Position the ball slightly back in the stance and stand with your bodyweight a little more on the left leg than on the right. Notice how close the ball is to the feet.

2 Move your arms, hands and club back together with no wrist break, keeping the clubhead low to the ground. The clubface should still be hooded.

3 Just before impact the club-head and shaft, and hands and arms, should return to the same position as in the address. Keep your body very still.

4 As you follow through your wrists should not move and you should keep the body quite still. The ball will fly away low to the ground.

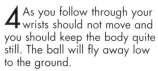

5 Move your arms and club towards the target as one unit. Take them forward at least as far as they went back on the backswing. During this action keep your legs still and shoulders square.

6 Watch the result.

CLOSE TO THE
PUTTING SURFACE

1 Look at the spot where you would like the ball to land and then run up to and in the hole.

2 Set the ball quite close to your feet and hold the grip of the club quite low down.

3 The action is a movement of the hands and arms, not the body. The clubhead should still be hooded and low to the ground.

4 Swing your arms and club together so that impact is slow and smooth. Keep you body still and shoulders square.

5 The clubhead should remain low to the ground as it moves towards the target. Do not cock your wrists. Keep your body and head still.

6 Follow through at least as far forward as you went back on the backswing.

1 Hold the grip of the club slightly further up than for the other chipping shots to help make a longer backswing. Feet, legs and hips open.

CHIPPING FROM FURTHER AWAY

2 Cock your wrists in order to swing the club further back and hit the ball a greater distance. Little to no body movement.

3 Bring the clubhead into the ball low to the ground.

4 Your club, hands and arms should be working smoothly together with your right leg and side moving towards the target. Some grass will be moved at impact.

5 Watch the result with the club-head and the ball still in line with one another. The ball is low and ready to run.

Key Points Card	
	Remarks
1	Always use the correct hold on the club.
2	Select the correct club and decide where you want the ball to land.
3	Keep the body still.
4	Use little to no wrist action.
5	Keep the clubhead low.
6	Swing the club backwards and forwards the same distance.

THE CHIP SHOT

The chip is a low running shot, therefore you need to take loft off the clubface. Select a club that has a comfortable length of shaft. At the address set your hands slightly ahead of the ball, this will deloft the club. The clubface is now hooded.

On the takeaway, there is no wrist break, the clubhead is still hooded, the body stays steady and the clubhead is low to the ground.

PUTTING

Putts are probably the most pressurized shots on the golf course. In no area is practice more important. Practise so that you feel confident with your putting action, able to judge distances and able to read the green. The importance of putting is illustrated by the old golfing phrase, 'You drives for show, but you putts for dough'.

PUTTING

Putting is an area of the game that is neglected by many club and higher handicap players. This may be because the green is an accessible part of the golf course and if you fail to putt the ball then 'all the world' can see. Very few people are prepared to spend time on the practice green and practice is what is usually required.

Confidence will come from good sound technique and practice. Always remember that however close you are to the hole, do not trust to luck. Take care to line up for the shot. Putting is never as easy as it looks.

1 The putter head is set square to the target with the ball in the centre of the clubface. A reverse overlap grip is being used and the arms are extended down. Ball positioned just left of centre in the stance, the body is evenly balanced. Head positioned over the ball.

2 At the takeaway the head and body are kept still as the club is taken back with a movement of the arms and shoulders. Try and avoid using wrist action when putting. Move the whole of the putter - the head, shaft and grip - with pendular movement of the arms.

3 On the follow-through the head and body are kept still, and the whole club swung with the arms, using no wrist break. How far the putter is taken back and through will depend on the length of the putt and the speed of the green.

Opposite: Justin Leonard.

81

BALL ALIGNMENT

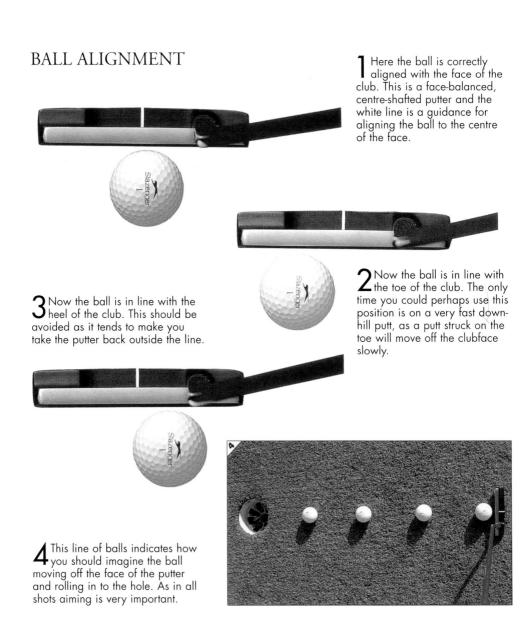

1 Here the ball is correctly aligned with the face of the club. This is a face-balanced, centre-shafted putter and the white line is a guidance for aligning the ball to the centre of the face.

2 Now the ball is in line with the toe of the club. The only time you could perhaps use this position is on a very fast downhill putt, as a putt struck on the toe will move off the clubface slowly.

3 Now the ball is in line with the heel of the club. This should be avoided as it tends to make you take the putter back outside the line.

4 This line of balls indicates how you should imagine the ball moving off the face of the putter and rolling in to the hole. As in all shots aiming is very important.

THE GRIP

1 Put both hands close together, with thumbs on the top of the grip and the index finger of your left hand outside the middle three fingers of your right hand. The index finger of the right hand should go down the grip.

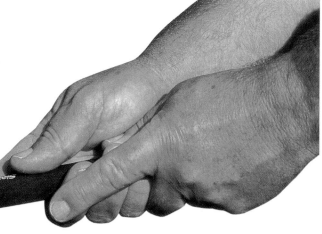

2 A different view of the hands. This is called the reverse overlap grip. Whichever way you hold the putter you must make sure it becomes part of your arm because a good putting action avoids independent wrist movement. The pressure of the grip should be quite soft.

3 Holding the head over the hole like this shows that the face of the club is square to the target, the hole.

THE ADDRESS

Keep the body out of the way to enable free movement of the putter back and through. Align the ball with the inside of the left shoe to create top spin and make the ball roll. Your head should be directly over the ball and hands held away and out from the legs. Body-weight is evenly balanced.

THE PROFESSIONALS

Bernhard Langer of Germany using a broomhandle putter.

BALL-TO-TARGET LINE

View from behind the line of the putt. The line of the feet and body is square with the ball-to-target line.

THE SHORT PUTT

The putt shown here is a good length to practise with. Given that putting is largely a question of confidence it is often better to practise with putts that you are likely to hole.

1 Hold the grip and check that the 'V' of your left hand is pointing to your left shoulder and that the 'V' of your right hand is pointing to your right shoulder. The address position is well-balanced and the ball lines up with the inside of your left shoe.

2 Take the putter low to the ground as one unit from your shoulders. The distance that the putter goes back will depend on the length of the shot and the speed of the green.

3 On contact do not create any wrist movement. Your head position should stay very still and there is no leg or hip movement.

4 On these short putts it is tempting to look at the hole as you stroke the putt, but continue concentrating on the shot.

THE LONG PUTT

1 Think of the distance you have to roll the ball for it to reach the hole.

2 Stroke the ball smoothly towards the hole with the arms and club.

3 Even when the golf ball is halfway to the hole your head should not have moved.

4 The only change in these two pictures has been the movement of the ball. The head has stayed still.

5 View of the follow-through. The putter reaching completion.

Key Points Card	
	Remarks
1	Check you have the correct grip.
2	The ball should be centred on the clubface.
3	The face of the club should be square to the target.
4	Putting is a shoulder and arms movement. No wrist action.
5	Keep your head still.

PUTTING PRACTICE

It is always best to practise on a level part of the green; once you can make the ball race straight on short distances then you will be able to cope with long putts and borrows in the greens.

The most important part of any putt is the first 9-12ins (230-300mm). If the shot starts correctly there is a good chance of success, but a putt that starts badly rarely improves.

Having lined the ball with the centre of the clubface practise making a smooth back and through swing. Depending on the speed and the length of the green the distance you have to swing the putter back will vary. As the length of putt increases the length of the swing will also increase and in so doing the putter will come back slightly on the inside.

1 You do not need a hole to practise this exercise. Take four balls and play the first one to an open area.

2 Repeat the same putt three or more times, get four balls to finish as close to one another as possible.

3 This exercise will help you practise the pace of the green and develop a consistent stroke.

HOLING SHORT PUTTS

Place four balls each a little further from the hole. Hole them, working from the one nearest to the hole. Start by testing yourself on a short putt and gradually move the balls further away.

SHAPING THE PUTT

The amount you have to allow for borrows on the green will depend on the texture of the grass, which in turn determines the speed of the green. The golden rule is that if you decide that you have to allow for the ball to move left or right because of the lie of the land, then you must endeavour to set the ball moving straight from the putter head and let the ground shape the putt. If the surface of the green is fast then you need to allow more into the borrow.

Always look from behind the ball to see what shape the putt is going to make.

Key Points Card	
	Remarks
1	Start by practising short putts.
2	Repeat the same length of putt several times to develop a consistent stroke.
3	Then practise putts moving further away.
4	If there are borrows in the green let the ground shape the putt.

THE ELEMENTS OF PUTTING

Address the ball with the face of the putter at right angles to the ground and the ball in line with your left heel. Strike the ball with an upward movement to cause top spin and roll. Keep the putter head quite low to the ground as it passes the left shoe. Having set your line and address you must stand quite still and stroke the ball and make it roll.

Opposite: Jose-Maria Olazabal.

HAZARDS AND DIFFICULT SHOTS

However good you are at golf there are bound to be times when you will find yourself in an awkward situation, whether it is under some trees, on a slope or in a bunker. In these cases it is often best not to be too ambitious, and you should concentrate on the job in hand - getting your ball back on to the fairway. Once there you can think about your next shot.

GREENSIDE BUNKER

1 Feet, legs, hips and shoulders open to the target. Position the ball just left of the centre in your stance. This will help you to present the full loft of the club to the target. Settle your feet in the sand, this will give you a firm stance and help you feel its consistency. Look at the sand about 2in (50mm) behind the ball. Use the standard hold on the club so that the clubface is open.

2 Take the club back and up with your hands and arms, and a responding shoulder, hip and leg movement. The amount of movement required will depend on how far you have to hit the shot. Notice how the club that is swung back is pointing in the same direction as the club aligned along the feet. This indicates that the club should move along the line of address position.

3 At the start of the downswing the clubhead has lots of loft and the face is visible. With this alignment and arm-swing, your swing should naturally go across the ball-to-target line. Keep your hands and arms together, working underneath the golf club.

4 Make contact with the sand about 2in (50mm) behind the ball. Head position very still. Move your legs and hips out of the way to help your shoulders keep the line they were set in at the address. The ball will move left of the target along the swing path of the club. But because you aimed the clubface at the target, and open to your stance, the ball will cut in its flight.

5 Your right leg, hip and shoulder move to help take the swing high on the follow-through. Keep your hold on the club and continue to swing along the open line set by your body at the address.

Key Points Card	
	Remarks
	Use a sand wedge with bounce.
2	Ball forward in the stance.
3	Look at the sand where you intend to hit.
4	Swing along the open shoulder line.
5	Follow through keeping loft on the clubface.

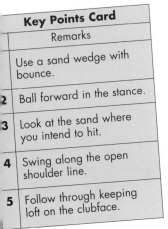

93

GREENSIDE BUNKER: EXAMPLE TWO

1 Ball slightly forward and clubhead above the sand.

2 The swing of the hands and arms taking the club back and up.

3 Body swinging under the head, arms extended with the hands keeping the loft on the face of the club.

4 Hands held high with the shoulders just bringing the head around.

5 Body pointing left of the target with a full follow-through.

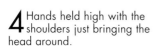

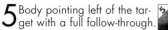

BALL BACK IN GREENSIDE BUNKER

1 Set the ball slightly left of centre in the stance and perhaps a little further away from your feet. Align your body to the left of the target.

2 Swing the club further back, making a fuller hip and shoulder turn. Make sure your arms and legs are working well together on the downswing. Wrists still cocked, head very still with plenty of room for the shoulders to move.

3 Less sand is taken. Your wrists and hands bring the loft of the club through the ball to send it high enough to cover the full distance of the sand.

4 Notice the high follow-through. Keep the top of your body tilted over the ground.

5 Turn your body completely to face to the left of the target and maintain your balance.

FRONT OF GREENSIDE BUNKER: BALL SAT DOWN

1 Stand in a relaxed address position, feet slightly open, shoulders square, the clubhead square to your shoulders and do not hold the club too tightly.

2 Take the club back with your hands and arms, with a little movement coming from your shoulders and hips.

3 Swing down to hit the sand several inches behind the ball.

4 Again head steady. You will hit lots of sand, but keep your arms and hands moving ahead of the golf club.

BALL ON FIRM SAND IN GREENSIDE BUNKER

1 This shot will need a smooth full swing, not taking too much sand.

2 Take the club back without such an early wrist break, for a shallower attack on the sand.

3 Relaxed body and arm-swing to the top of the backswing.

4 Slip the club under the ball slowly.

5 Good release of the clubhead.

6 Make a relaxed full follow-through.

BALL ON THE UP-SLOPE

1 Position the ball slightly left of centre. Set your body perpendicular to slope. Widen the stance and flex your knees.

3 Maintain your balance and angle set at the address. Take the club back and up with your hands and arms.

2 As with all these bunker shots keep your head steady.

4 Your legs should hold your body on to the slope. Swing the club to the ball with the top of your body.

5 Because your legs are working to hold your body on the slope, the hip movement through will be at a minimum causing a restricted follow-through.

BALL PLUGGED

1 The clubface is in a closed position and the grip is correct. Stance is square. The ball centred between feet. Feet set firmly in the sand.

2 Look at the sand several inches behind the ball. Set off on a smooth full swing.

3 At the top of backswing make a good shoulder turn. The clubface is still closed.

4 Work with your legs and hips keeping your arms down ready to hit a lot of sand.

5 Lots of sand will be hit. The weight of the sand will open the clubhead. This is why you set the clubface closed.

6 Make every effort to follow through, but this is often hard. Getting the ball out of the bunker is about the best that you can hope for.

BALL IN A FAIRWAY BUNKER

1 Set your feet firmly in the sand. If your feet sink, shorten the length of the club you are using. Set the ball in the centre of your stance.

2 As you take the clubhead up and away from the ball, look at the top of the ball and firm up your hold.

3 The firm hold on the club will restrict your wrist action. Take the club back with your body.

4 Full backswing, good shoulder turn and the club pointing parallel to the target as your body is set square to the ball-to-target line.

5 Your body-weight should be on your left side. Hands and arms ready to take the ball before you hit the sand.

7 A well-balanced follow-through and the arms are now folded.

6 Hold your head steady, take the ball quite cleanly off the sand. Your hands and arms release the club with your arms together.

101

FAIRWAY BUNKER: EXAMPLE TWO

3 At impact you will first strike the ball, then a little sand. Swing the club past the body.

1 Embed your feet slightly to give a firm stance.

2 Your body and arms work together as you complete the backswing.

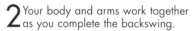

4 High follow-through, body facing the target.

THE PROFESSIONALS

Nick Faldo of England playing from a greenside bunker. Here you can see clearly that the loft on the clubface has thrown the ball up and out of the bunker.

Key Points Card

	Remarks
1	Choose the club with enough loft to get over the lip of the bunker.
2	Keep a firm hold on the club.
3	Look at the top of the ball.
4	Make a smooth, balanced swing.

BALL ON AN UPHILL LIE

Do not be ambitious on sloping lies. The uphill lie is difficult. The main thing you have to work out is how to make the clubhead swing down and up the slope. To do this you have to set your body at right angles to the hill. This will make the golf club more lofted, so select a less lofted club. The action you are going to make will tend to hook the ball, so aim right of your intended target.

1 In setting the angle of your spine at right angles to the slope bend your left leg slightly more than usual.

2 This will restrict the movement of your hips through impact and is likely to make your hands more active and inclined to cross over.

Key Points Card	
	Remarks
1	The club you select will depend on the severity of the slope.
2	Both hands work together.
3	Hold the grip with the last three fingers of the right hand.
4	Play the ball off your left (higher) leg.

3 Play the ball off your higher leg. This will help in setting your spinal angle and will give you room to swing the clubhead down and up the slope.

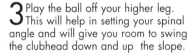

4 The angle that the body was set to the slope at the address has been maintained.

BALL ON A DOWNHILL LIE

The downhill lie is probably the most difficult of all hazardous shots. In the set-up stand so that it is possible to swing the club up and down the slope. You have to position the ball back from the centre of your stance and incline your body down the slope to make your spine vertical to the angle of the ball. Doing this will cancel the angle of loft on the clubface so select a more lofted club.

1 Position the ball back from the centre of the stance.

2 You will now be bent into the slope and it will be difficult to make a complete body turn. The backswing will not be as complete as normal.

3 To take the ball cleanly off the ground keep the club low to the ground as it goes through impact.

4 Make every effort to keep your hands ahead of the clubhead when striking the ball.

5 Make a shortened follow-through and the ball should fly away low and straight.

BALL BELOW YOUR FEET

When the ball is below your feet the tendency is for the hands to roll the clubface open. Consequently, you are likely to send the ball swerving from left to right. The best way to play this shot will result in the ball flying high and only a short distance. You must accept this, rather than trying to play a more ambitious shot.

1 Ensure that you use the full length of the golf club. Hold the grip near the end.

2 Set the ball forward in your stance. Aim left of your target. Put more weight on your heels to avoid falling down the slope.

3 On the takeaway do not fight the slope. Use less body movement, and swing with your hands and arms.

4 Keep your balance as you hit the shot, let the club come down to impact with an open face.

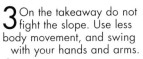

5 Do not try and close it - this will result in you falling down the slope and fluffing the shot. Your follow-through will be restricted.

BALL ABOVE YOUR FEET

When the ball is above your feet the tendency is for the ball to hook. When you place the club to the ball the clubface will be facing to the left of your target. Also with the ball above your feet your swing plane becomes flatter.

1 Aim to the right of your intended target.

2 Hold the grip of the club several inches down from the top. If you use the full length of the club you risk hitting the ground before the ball. Set your body-weight into the slope to prevent falling backwards when you swing the club back and through.

3 The swing must be a smooth body and arm movement, without a lot of hand action.

4 The arm-swing has been flattened by the lie of the ball above the feet.

5 At impact, because of the danger of the slope, play with a lot of hand action. But note this closes the face of the club severely causing the shot to be smothered.

6 Well-balanced, with a flat follow-through showing how the club and swing accommodate the slope.

Key Points Card	
	Remarks
1	Play with the ball in the middle of your stance.
2	Hold down the grip several inches.
3	Aim slightly right of the target to allow for the hook.
4	Set your balance into the slope.
5	Do not resist the angle of the slope.
6	Keep the swing smooth.

HIGH SHOTS OVER TREES

You may find yourself in the unfortunate position of having to play this rather awkward shot. It often pays not to be too ambitious and simply get the ball back into a playing position. In this case the ball missed the fairway to the left and there are some large trees in the way. Club selection is vital. The most important consideration is to have enough height to clear the trees.

1 Set the ball forward in your stance, make sure your grip pressure is not too tight and think hard about the shot you are going to make.

2 At impact your shoulders should be very square and your head well back. The ball sets off in an upward lift.

3 The whole movement suggests the ball is being hit forward and up into the air.

4 Remain well-balanced, holding your body under the shot, turn your head and look underneath the ball.

LOW SHOTS IN BUSHES

1 f you need to restrict the backswing separate your hands from one another. Exactly how far apart you place them will depend on how far back you can take the club. You may need to bend low to get under the branches. Position the ball back in the stance to make impact earlier.

DIFFICULT SHOTS

When the ball has to be lofted quickly, for example over a mound or out of a deep bunker, set the clubface open.

When you follow through playing from a greenside bunker or any high shot, hit through the ball and keep the loft on the club.

2 The arms take the club back and the body-weight remains still to avoid hitting the branches.

3 Impact is made with the right hand and arms, and the head is kept very still. The ball is now out on the fairway.

LOW SHOTS UNDER TREES

1 Position the ball slightly back in the stance. Make sure the left hand is still in line with the inside of your left leg. The head of the club will be slightly hooded if the leading edge is square to the target line. Flex your right leg inwards at the knee, settling your weight slightly on to your left side.

2 Swing the club back and up with your arms and hands. Your weight should not move to the right.

3 Keep your head still as your arms and legs pull the club down. Hips square to the target line and shoulders back

4 Keep your body low and punch the ball away with your forearms.

EXAMPLE TWO

1 The same shot from behind the ball. From this position you can see how the ball must fly low.

2 The shoulders help the arms take the club back and the legs are flexed.

3 The hands maintain a firm hold of the club, arms working closely together.

4 The right shoulder moves down and through.

Key Points Card	
	Remarks
1	Ball back slightly in the address.
2	Keep the leading edge of the club square, deloft (hood) the club.
3	As you strike the ball keep your hands and arms ahead of the club.
4	Keep your head still.

THE PROFESSIONALS

Bernhard Langer of Germany having to punch the ball out of heavy rough with a lofted club. You can see here that he is using an interlocking grip.

Opposite: Greg Norman.

FAULTS AND PROBLEM SOLVING

If a golf ball is hit correctly it will fly straight towards the target. Shots that deviate to the left or right have been wrongly struck. The faults can be many and may be in your aim, your grip, your stance and your swing. In this chapter the pictures with pink shirts are the ones where errors are being shown and the white shirts show the correct action.

SLICING

The slice is a ball that swings from left to right in its flight and is caused by an open address position. This leads to an out-to-in swing path and the clubface being open to this swing path. The ball starts off flying on the swing path - to the left - but the open clubface puts spin on the ball and so it swerves round to the right.

The clubs on the ground indicate parallel lines to the centre of the fairway, highlighting the open stance. In most cases players are not aware that they are making this error.

FRONT VIEW

1 Open Set-up. The ball is a long way forward in the stance and the head is over the ball. The 'V's on both hands are pointing to the left shoulder causing an open clubface.

2 The forward position of the ball and the open shoulders have restricted the shoulder turn. The club is now pointing left with the face open.

3 At impact the body is open, The hands are forward and the club is open to the body.

4 The club is travelling on the inside. The head is well forward, but there has been no release of the clubhead.

5 The follow-through is well left of the fairway and the clubhead is being held open by the hands.

SLICING: EXAMPLE TWO

1 This gives a clear view of a very open stance and alignment. The clubs on the ground indicate parallel lines to the centre of the fairway.

2 Because of the open address, the arms have swung the club to the left of the target. In doing this the club was taken back on the outside and is now all set to swing down on the outside.

3 At impact, the shoulders and hips turn to the left of the target taking the arms inside the ball-to-target line. The hands have now turned the clubface open to the swing path.

4 The clubhead moves through impact onto the inside path. The clubface is open therefore the ball will start flying left. But the open clubface puts spin on the ball, so it will swerve to the right in flight.

5 The head and shoulders are now well forward, the hands have not released the clubhead. The body is facing well left of the fairway.

PULLING

A pull is a shot that sends the ball flying straight to the left. It has the same swing path as the slice - out-to-in - but a different shaped clubhead at impact. The clubface is square at impact.

1 Notice how the set-up is the same as the set-up for the slice.

2 The swing is along the line of the body. The club is 'laid off' - pointing to the left of the target.

5 The follow-through shows that the clubhead was released along the out-to-in swing path.

4 After impact the club is well over to the left, covering the ground called the inside. The ball is going left and stays left.

3 In the downswing you can see the club is about to travel down on the outside.

HOOKING

A hook is the opposite shot to the slice, it sends the ball from right to left. The swing path is in-to-out, so the ball starts to the right following the swing path, but because the clubhead is closed at impact the ball spins round to the left. The hook is caused by errors in the set-up which in turn affect the swing plane and swing path.

1 The whole alignment is facing well to the right of the centre of the fairway, showing a closed stance. This is opposite to the slice. On the takeaway the club will travel on the outside.

2 At the top of the back-swing the club is pointing along the closed shoulder line, to the right of the target. This is known as being 'across the line'. The clubhead is closing, the clubface is facing the sky.

3 The downswing comes in very much on the inside, keeping the right side well back.

4 The club is moving on a swing path to the outside. The ball starts going to the right but spins off to the left.

5 The body is in the way so the arms are struggling to make a proper follow-through.

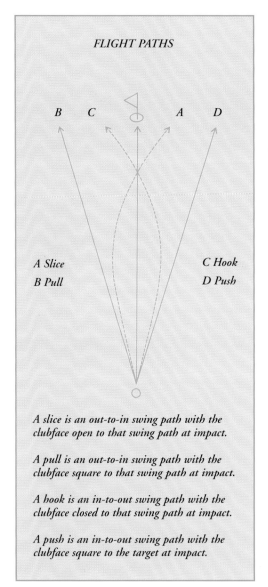

FLIGHT PATHS

A Slice
B Pull

C Hook
D Push

A slice is an out-to-in swing path with the clubface open to that swing path at impact.

A pull is an out-to-in swing path with the clubface square to that swing path at impact.

A hook is an in-to-out swing path with the clubface closed to that swing path at impact.

A push is an in-to-out swing path with the clubface square to the target at impact.

FRONT VIEW

1 The ball is set back. The feet, knees, hips and shoulders are aiming to the right and both 'V's are pointing more to the right shoulder.

2 At the top of the backswing, notice the closed clubface and how the club points across the line of the club on the ground.

3 The ball is hit from the inside. The right shoulder is well back and not helping the club through at impact.

THE PROFESSIONALS

Severiano Ballesteros of Spain recovering from a hook into rough grass. With his swashbuckling style Ballesteros is a master at dealing with awkward lies and bunkers.

4 The hands have turned the face over causing the hook. The ball will swerve to the left.

5 The fact that the right side was not helping the club through at impact shows now in the follow-through.

PUSHING

A push is the opposite shot to the pull, it sends the ball flying straight to the right. It has the same swing path as the hook - in-to-out - but the ball starts to the right, and stays there.

1 The alignment is facing well to the right. This is a closed stance.

2 The club is pointing across the line and the clubface is closed.

4 Impact is in-to-out and the clubface is square to the swing path. The ball starts right and flies straight along this line.

3 This results in the attack on the ball being too much from the inside.

5 The ball was hit straight down the right side of the course.

PUSHING: EXAMPLE TWO

1 The set-up is facing to the right of target. The ball is well back in the stance, so the takeaway will go back quickly on the inside. This shot could be either a hook or a push.

3 The swing path is on the inside and the clubface is square. The shot is a push. The ball goes right.

2 The club closes at the top of the backswing. The shot could still be a hook or a push.

4 Because of the in-to-out swing path, the body is in the way of the follow-through and cannot clear.

TOPPING

This is the type of mistake that you are inclined to make when you are starting to play golf and have not learned to trust your movements. Note how the upward action has been made either with the body or the club-head. This is incorrect as it is the loft on the face of the club that sends the ball in the air.

1 At the address the set-up is square and the posture is good. Everything looks ready.

2 The club was swung to a good position by the hands and arms, but the legs have straightened causing the posture to rise.

3 Just before impact. Sadly the legs and back have not recovered the angles that were set at the address. The hands and arms are trying to find the ball.

4 Everything except the ball is going up.

TOPPING:
EXAMPLE TWO

1 The feet are a little closed and shoulders just a touch open. The head position is not set for a good shoulder pivot.

2 The head has to move to the right to allow for the shoulder turn. This causes the body to sway to the right as the arms and hands go back and up.

3 The body is still far back on the right leg.

4 The ball is topped. The right side never helped the down and through swing. The club was rising up on the ball at impact.

TOPPING: EXAMPLE THREE

1 All is set for the ball to be smashed straight down the middle, but the legs are possibly a little straight.

2 By now the legs are rather bent causing a loss of height, but a top could still be avoided.

3 The body is moving up again, but there is still a chance of striking the ball in the correct place.

4 But the legs have straightened again, causing the top.

FLUFFING

The fluff is a shot where the club hits the ground before it hits the ball. As with topping, the problems often arise because of an incorrect position at the address.

1 The address is looking good except that the golf ball is too far back. This may mean that the body-weight is incorrectly distributed.

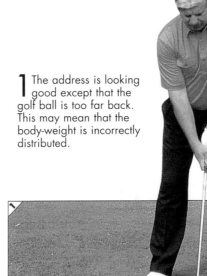

2 At the top of the backswing the club is back in a very upright manner. Little or no weight is transferred to the right side.

3 On the downswing you can see the result of the ball being too far back. The head is now too far forward, leaving no room to get a clean strike at the ball.

4 Because of the steepness of the angle of attack the clubhead hit the ground.

FLUFFING:
EXAMPLE TWO

1 The stance is a little closed which means the ball will be too far back.

2 The club has been swung back outside the ball-to-target line, creating an upright position.

3 The bottom of the swing arrived too early, hence the amount of ground being moved.

4 The arms create a restricted follow through due to the upright position.

FLUFFING: EXAMPLE THREE

1 The ball is teed-up correctly, but the shoulders are set slightly open to the feet and hips.

2 Because the top half of the body has lifted the club up to the top of the backswing, the right leg is very straight and the angle of the spine has been altered from the address.

3 On the downswing, the legs and body make a great effort to return to the level set at the address so that the ball can be taken off the tee.

4 The body continued to go down and the club hits the ground in front of the ball.

131

OVER-SWINGING

The over-swing is a common error. Whilst you notice it mainly at the top of the backswing, the next set of pictures demonstrate that the faults can actually be seen right at the beginning of the swing.

ARM-SWING AND BODY TURN

1 The club is well on its way to the backswing. It has clearly been taken back with virtually no help from the body. As a result the left arm has started to bend at the elbow. The club was taken back too far, too fast, too soon.

2 The body has not caught up with the club. Now the left arm is a little more bent, the arms are further apart, and the head and shaft of the club have gone beyond the horizontal line.

3 The arms separated at the top of the backswing. At this stage recovery can still be made but it will be difficult.

4 The splayed formation of the arms on the follow-through which suggests that the complete recovery was not made.

ERROR: EXAMPLE TWO

1 The ball and clubhead were set on the ball-to-target line at the address, with the feet, hips and shoulders parallel to this line. The body is making a good pivoting movement, but the arms and club have come up to join the body. Because of this the club moved slightly inside the ball-to-target line.

2 The same action from the front. Despite the good body movements the arms have brought the club up flat to the body losing the alignment to the target.

ERROR: EXAMPLE THREE

1 Again the clubhead and ball were set square to the target at the address. But only the arms have taken the club up, and in so doing it has gone slightly on the outside of the ball-to-target line.

2 The same action from the front. The body has moved side-ways and the head and shoulders are down. This is an arm-swing without the correct body turn.

THE CORRECT SWING

The first picture shows the start of the backswing from an address position that was square to the ball-to-target line. The clubhead and shaft have been taken to about waist height with a turning movement of the left shoulder, left hip and a swinging movement of the left arm and the whole of the club.

Take note that the hands and the face of the club have worked together without any independent wrist movement, also that the left arm and the club are now parallel to the ball-to-target line. This one piece movement has brought the club slightly on the inside of the target line.

The 'V'-shapes of the hands are still pointing between the face and right shoulder.

This second picture shows the same position from the front. Some weight has been transferred on to the instep of the right foot. The right leg has kept its position which will create the hip turn. The position of the head and spinal angle have been maintained. The arms and club have remained the same distance apart as they were at the address.

The hands and clubface have moved together. Controlling the shape of the clubhead and its direction at the start of the backswing is of great importance. This is one-piece takeaway.

Opposite: Tiger Woods.

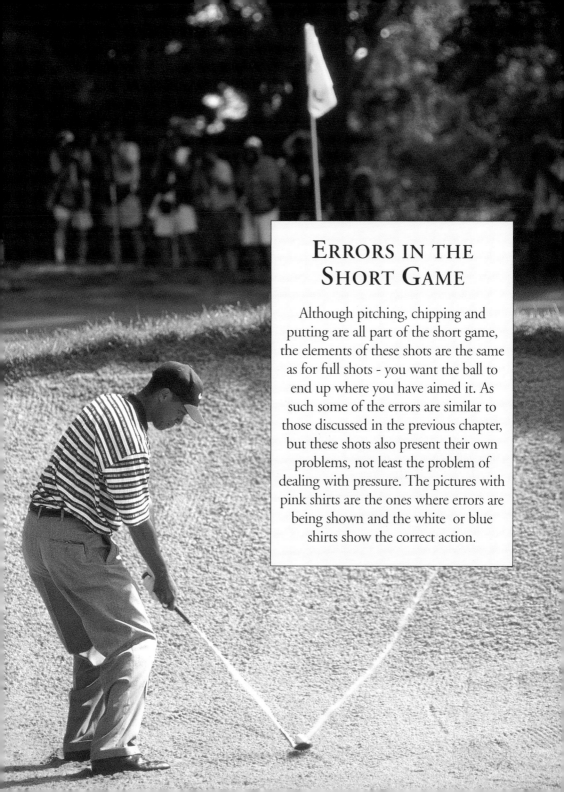

ERRORS IN THE SHORT GAME

Although pitching, chipping and putting are all part of the short game, the elements of these shots are the same as for full shots - you want the ball to end up where you have aimed it. As such some of the errors are similar to those discussed in the previous chapter, but these shots also present their own problems, not least the problem of dealing with pressure. The pictures with pink shirts are the ones where errors are being shown and the white or blue shirts show the correct action.

ERRORS IN PITCHING

The pitch is a shot used to hit the ball straight in the air. Therefore, you must first select the club with loft on it such as a 9-iron, wedge or sand wedge. These will give you the height on the shot that you need. As in all shots, for the pitch you start by lining up the leading edge of the club square to the target. It should be at right angles to the ball-to-target line.

TOPPING

1 It is tempting to imagine that leaning back will lift the ball up and over the bunker. But this ignores the fact that it is the loft on the club that sends the ball into the air.

2 In this address position the club will be taken back with the hands and wrists holding on to the club not letting the wrists cock. Also see how the head has moved to the left, perhaps with the idea that it should be kept down.

3 Contact is made with the leading edge of the club so the ball is hit into the bunker. See how all the effort seems to be going into lifting the ball up in the air. The head is to the right, the hands have stopped and the clubhead is up in the air, causing impact to be halfway up the side of the ball. The left heel is off the ground, which is helping to make a lifting action.

4 This detail shows the position of the club at impact. There is no loft on this part of the club. You should strike the ball in the centre of the clubface.

5 In the completed swing the body is well back, with the left foot more off the ground and the arms and hands still trying to lift the ball over the bunker.

FLUFFING

1 The miscalculation here is the belief that if you take a lofted club and hit down at the ball it will go into the air. In truth, standing like this will probably take loft off the clubface.

2 The club is taken up and back quite severely with the hands and arms. You can see more clear here how far ahead of the ball the player is standing.

3 The ground has been hit before the ball. The ball is airborne but it will not make the distance required because it was hit too far up the clubface. This part of the club does not propel the ball forward with any speed.

4 Due to the steep angle of attack, the follow-through is very restricted. This is a good example of the loft on the clubface not being used correctly..

THE SOCKET

1 The hands and arms have taken the club back too far on the inside of the ball-to-target line.

2 The wrists are too cocked, taking the club too far back. If the clubhead is brought straight down from this position the swing path will be in-to-out, and the ball will fly to the right.

3 An attempt is made to correct the backswing. The shoulders have turned but at impact the clubhead is slightly further away from the body. The heel of the club, the socket, collides with the ball.

4 The position of the clubhead at impact.

5 The body has come up because the club and arms swung out and around on the downswing, and at impact.

FLUFFING

1 Comfortable address, clubhead and ball aiming at the target.

2 Hands and arms take the club straight back and up.

3 Impact, then the club and arms swing towards the flag.

4 The right side helps the movement to the target

5 The weight is on the left side in a well-balanced follow-through.

ERRORS IN CHIPPING

The chip is a shot that can be played with the putter if the ground between the ball and the green is clean and fast. The chip must travel straight and on a low trajectory. When chipping you must avoid opening and closing the clubhead during the swing. The stroke needs to be played without wrist action so that the clubhead can be kept close to the shot. It is very similar to the putt.

1 A medium iron has been selected and the address position is looking good.

2 This is where the mistake occurs. There appears to have been a change of plan - the hands and wrists have taken the clubhead back into an open position.

3 At impact, the hands roll the clubface back to the ball closing the head and overcompensating for the open face on the backswing.

4 The clubhead continues in this rolling manner sending the ball too far and to the left.

2 On the backswing, the clubhead has not stayed low to the ground. It now has too much loft for this shot.

ERROR: EXAMPLE TWO

1 The ball is lying well on the fairway, just short of the apron of the green. A medium iron has been chosen for this chip and run shot. The hands are too far back and behind the ball. Also the body-weight is incorrect. It should be set slightly more on the left leg.

3 Only the right hand and arm have been used to bring the club to the impact area causing the clubhead to rise when it strikes the ball and therefore, topping it.

4 Further on through the shot, the clubhead is a long way from the ground. The left hand and arm stopped when the strike was made. On this occasion the ball will probably shoot right across the green.

CORRECT CHIP

When you want a low shot, keep the clubhead low to the ground on both the back and through swing.

1 Hands down the grip; leading edge square; well-balanced address.

2 Just before impact the body is still and the left hand and shaft together. Clubhead delofted.

3 At impact the arms and club return together to the ball. The clubhead is low to the ground.

4 Now the ball is on its way, flying low. The hands and arms have kept the clubhead low.

5 The body is well-balanced; the ball is about to land and then roll up to the flag.

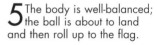

ERRORS IN PUTTING

You must make sure that the ball starts along the correct line. Remember that you must align the ball with the centre of the club-head, and set the ball in a position that enables you to take the putter back smoothly, low to the ground. The fewer movements you make with your hands and wrists when taking the clubhead backwards and forwards, the better.

1 The ball is lined up with the toe of the putter. This may cause the ball to roll to the right, and very often short.

2 The golf ball is in line with the heel of the putter. This will hit the ball left of the target.

1 Here the body is set square to the hole, but the head is not over the line of the putt. The hands are also a little low, with the ball too far away.

2 The hands and arms have taken the putter back from the ball, outside the ball-to-hole line. A good putting action would have taken the putter back along the ball-to-hole line. On a longer putt it would have gone slightly on the inside

3 Just before impact, you can see the putter head on the line of the target. The ball will be struck with the heel of the putter.

4 The putter head is well to the left of the hole, the hands have tried to square up the clubface. This action causes missed putts from all lengths.

145

ERROR: EXAMPLE TWO

1 The set-up appears to be aiming to the right of the hole, with the golf ball displaced towards the toe of the putter.

2 As the putter head is just about to make contact, see how the putter face is now aiming very much to the right, so the clubface is open to the hole. There is not much chance of the ball rolling towards the hole.

3 The swing of the putter head back and through was in no way able to send the ball to the hole.

4 The ball continues to move away from the hole.

2 The result of this address position is that the action at the start of the stroke is made by the wrists, They almost pick the putter head up.

ERROR: EXAMPLE THREE

1 The golf ball is a long way back in the stance. Therefore, the face of the putter cannot be at right angles to the ground.

THE PROFESSIONALS

Bernhard Langer of Germany having missed a putt at Kiawah, South Carolina, during the 1991 Ryder Cup. This tragedy at the final hole cost the European team the trophy.

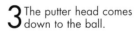

3 The putter head comes down to the ball.

4 It hits the ground as it strikes the ball and comes to a stop.

ERROR: EXAMPLE FOUR

1 See here how the shaft of the putter comes straight up, the forearms splay out and the elbows are bent. Having set this angle for the shaft of the club and the arms, it must be kept the same if you are to make a smooth stroke.

2 As the putter went back the hands went forward to the hole. This changes the way the arms are set compared to their position at the address. The shaft and left arm are now in line with one another.

3 An effort has been made to take the left hand and arm back to their position in the address. Now the right arm and the putter are in line.

4 The whole action is loose and wristy causing very poor contact on the ball.

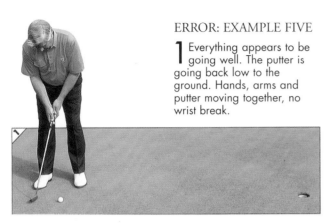

ERROR: EXAMPLE FIVE

1 Everything appears to be going well. The putter is going back low to the ground. Hands, arms and putter moving together, no wrist break.

2 The putter has reached the right point in the backswing for this length of putt. But what you cannot see on looking at this picture is that the golfer can see the hole out of the corner of his left eye.

3 The moment the ball was played the player started to look at the hole, causing the shoulders to turn and brake the forward momentum of the clubhead towards the hole.

4 Now he will have to will the ball to keep moving.

149

ERROR: EXAMPLE SIX

1&2 Again the error here is that the head has moved. Practise these short putts keeping your head still and listening for the ball to go into the hole.

3 Here you can see that the head is still with the shoulders square.

ERROR: EXAMPLE SEVEN

1–3 Here the head has kept still but far too much hand and wrist action has been used.

4 Here the hands, arms and putter are all working together.

151

RULES AND ETIQUETTE

With the increasing popularity
of golf, courses are becoming more
crowded and it is therefore all the
more important that you are
considerate to other players at all
times. In this chapter the basic rules
of the game and type of matches
you might like to play are examined.
But always check the local rules
before you start to play.

TYPES OF MATCHES

MATCH-PLAY

Match-play is a hole by hole contest. The scores are worked out according to how many holes each player wins or loses. For example, if after 16 holes player A has won three holes more than player B he or she cannot lose. Player A would have won the match 3&2 (three holes up, and only two to play). The most any player can win by is 10&8. Should the match be all square after 18 holes this could be what is called a halved match, but if a result is required the players will move to the first hole and start again until someone wins a hole. If player A wins the first extra hole the result will read that he won at the 19th.

STROKE-PLAY (MEDAL-PLAY)

In stroke-play you count the total strokes for the round. One round is 18 holes.

STABLEFORD

This a format of play where you score points. Points are awarded according to how many strokes under or over par the player takes at each hole. The total number of points scored at each hole added together gives the score.

Par+2 (Double bogey)	0pts
Par+1 (Bogey)	1pt
Par	2pts
Par–1 (Birdie)	3pts
Par–2 (Eagle)	4pts
Par–3 (Albatross)	5pts

FOURSOME

Foursome is a partnership game in which players take alternate shots with the same ball. The golfer who plays from the first tee drives at all the odd numbered holes and their partner tees off on the even numbered holes. This game can be played as either match-play, stroke-play or stableford against two other players.

Nowhere in the world is golf becoming more popular than in Japan. Golfing ranges provide golfers who live in the city with a chance to practise.

Opposite: Robertson and Old Tom Morris

FOUR BALL

Four ball is another partnership game. This time two players play the better of their two balls against the better ball of their opponents. This is a form of match-play. You can also have a four ball better ball stroke-play or stableford. The four ball method of play is perhaps the most popular, but its biggest drawback is that it can take rather a long time to complete a round.

THREE BALL AND THREESOME

The three ball is a match where each player plays against one another. The threesome is a match with one player playing their ball against two partners playing alternate shots with one ball.

THE SCORE CARD

Each player is responsible for their own score card even though the score is kept by the other players. There is a space for each player to record their own score as a marker. Never sign your own card if the score is incorrect. Always see that the correct handicap is shown on the card and the number of strokes received. Each player should check their hole by hole score and their gross and nett total.

A scorecard from the Royal Birkdale Golf Club

The Tented Village at the British Open, 1992.

THE PAR

The par of the course is made up by the yardage or metres of each hole.

Yards	Metres	Par
0-250	0-229	3
251-475	230-434	4
476+	435+	5

STROKE INDEX

The playing difficulty of each hole, as assessed by the club, is taken into account and a stroke index is allocated to each hole (see under handicap for further details).

TEE POSITIONS

Where possible each club will have the following tee positions permanently marked and measured: Ladies Medal Tees - Red; Mens Forward Tees - Yellow; Mens Medal Tees - White.

Colin Montgomerie during the play off against Steve Elkington for the US PGA at Riviera, Los Angeles in 1995. Elkington won at the first extra hole.

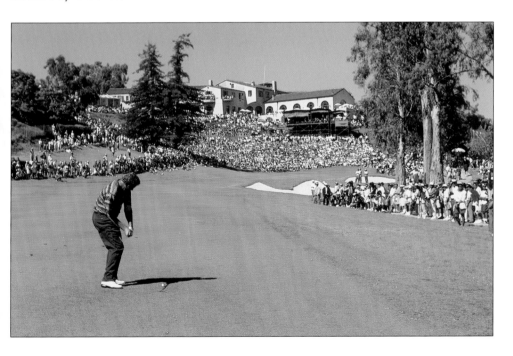

HANDICAPS

Handicapping is a system whereby strokes are subtracted from the scores of weaker players to enable golfers of different standards to compete fairly against one another. Handicaps are issued by golf clubs and authorized amateur golf associations.

HANDICAP ALLOWANCES

MATCH-PLAY

In match-play the handicap allowance is worked out as ¾ of the difference between the players handicaps. For example, if a player A is a 25 handicap and player B is a 10 handicap, the difference is 15. Three-quarters of 15 is 11¼, therefore, player A receives 11 strokes. These are taken at the holes where the figure 11 and under appears on the stroke index on the score card. If the difference does not come out to a whole number it is rounded up.

STROKE-PLAY (MEDAL-PLAY)

In stroke play you must complete every hole, then the whole handicap is deducted from the total score of the 18 holes completed. If the total score is 90, or less a handicap of 15, the score is 75.

SINGLE STABLEFORD

The allowance for single stableford is ⅞ths of the total handicap. For example, if the player has a handicap of 19, ⅞ths of 19 is 16.625, this is rounded up to 17. These strokes are taken at the holes where 17 and below are shown on the stroke index.

FOUR BALL MATCH-PLAY

Each player receives ¾ of the difference in handicap taken from the lowest handicap of the four players. The strokes are taken at the holes indicated on the stroke index.

FOURSOME MATCH-PLAY

In foursome match-play, add together the handicap of each partnership.

Tiger Woods, at 21, became the youngest winner of the Masters at Augusta in 1997.

FOURSOME STABLEFORD
Each pairing receives ⁷⁄₁₆ of their combined handicap; these strokes are taken at the holes indicated on the stroke index.

FOURSOME STROKE-PLAY
Each pairing received ½ of their combined handicap, this is then taken from their gross score for the completed 18 holes.

Golf is a game of world-wide popularity. This is the 18th green at Monastir, Tunisia.

FOURSOME STABLEFORD BETTER-BALL
Each player receives ⅞ths of their handicap. These strokes are taken at the holes indicated on the stroke index. The better ball of the two players is the score for each hole. Total points recorded is the team score.

FOUR BALL BETTER-BALL STROKE-PLAY
Each player receives ¾ of their handicap. Each pair then records their best gross and nett score for each hole, using the stroke index, the best nett score on each hole will be the pairings score.

RULES

There are a universal set of rules for golf that are constantly reviewed by the Royal and Ancient Golf Club of St Andrews and in America by the United States Golf Association. Outlined below are some of the most important rules, but always check to see if a club has any special rules of its own.

STARTING OUT

Before play commences announce to your opponent the number and make of the ball you are going to start with.

You are only permitted to have fourteen clubs in your bag. They do not have to be different clubs, two putters and several different wedges are acceptable. Penalties are incurred for carrying more clubs. For stroke-play two penalty strokes are given on each hole on which the violation occurred, with a maximum penalty of four strokes. In match-play you lose the hole on which the violation occurred, with a maximum penalty per round of the loss of two holes. When playing stableford deduct two points from the final tally for each hole on which a violation occurred, maximum deduction four points.

THE HONOUR
Who is going to hit the ball first? This is called the honour. If it is an organized competition the honour is taken by the player whose name appears first for that game. Otherwise decide by tossing a coin.

THE TEEING GROUND
This is a flat prepared area, which will have two tee markers on it. The tee of the day is a rectangle extending back two club lengths from a line between the markers. The ball must be teed-up within this area although you may stand outside if you wish.

In match-play if you tee-up from outside the teeing ground your opponent can ask you to take it again but there is no penalty. In stroke-play you are penalized by two strokes and must then play from within the teeing ground. Strokes played from outside the teeing ground do not count. If you fail to return to the tee before you tee-off on the next hole, or leave the 18th green you are disqualified.

158   *A modern set of irons.*

BALL FALLING OFF THE TEE PEG
This happens quite frequently. Even if the ball is teed-up in the correct way it may fall off of the tee at the address, or you may touch it with the clubhead and knock it off the tee. There is no penalty, replace the ball and play again. However, if you have started your downswing and you are unable to check before impact, making a glancing blow on the ball or even missing it, this counts as a stroke. You cannot replace the ball on the tee peg. Should you be able to stop your down-swing this does not constitute a stroke.

BALL IN PLAY

Once the game has begun the ball must be played as it lies, which means that you cannot touch it or improve its lie. Some courses do have a local rule which permits you to move the ball, often during the winter, when the preferred lie rule can be introduced. The preferred lie rule entitles you to pick up the ball and replace it within 6 in (152mm) of its original position, but it cannot be placed closer to the hole. If the ball comes to rest in casual water, it has to be dropped in accordance with the rules.

During the playing of each hole you are not permitted to play any practice strokes. A stroke is defined as the forward movement of the club with the intention of striking the ball. It is quite in order to have practice swings but when doing this do not cause damage to the turf, also do not hold up play.

Below: Dead leaves and twigs being moved from around the ball. This is quite in order as long as you do not move the ball. But you cannot break off any vegetation that is growing.

PLAYING THE WRONG BALL

Always make sure the ball you are about to play is your own; should you play the wrong ball you incur penalties. In match-play, you lose the hole. In stroke-play, add a two-stroke penalty and then play your own ball. If the ball you played belongs to a fellow competitor it must be replaced. The penalties do not apply if you are playing in a hazard.

LOST BALL

If your ball is lost you are allowed five minutes to look for it. Whenever this happens always tell the match behind you to play through. In match-and stroke-play, if after five minutes you cannot find the ball go back to where you played your last shot. If it was on the tee, tee-up a new ball, and if it was on the fairway or in the rough drop a new ball as near as possible to the spot where you played your last stroke. Add a penalty shot and lose the distance the ball went, for example, if your ball is lost from the tee shot your next shot will be counted as your third. This is known as stroke and distance.

BALL UNFIT FOR PLAY

If the ball is visibly damaged,by a cut or a crack, or has gone out of shape so that its true flight or roll is affected you can replace it without penalty. Make sure you consult your opponent or marker. This does not apply for mud stuck to the side of the ball or if the paint is scratched.

BALL OUT OF BOUNDS

As with the lost ball, you apply the stroke and distance rule. Go back to where you played your last shot and add a penalty shot. Check the score card for out of bounds areas. It is the club's duty to define its boundaries. You can stand out of bounds to hit a ball that is in bounds.

DROPPING THE BALL

Stand upright and hold the ball at shoulder height. Drop the ball. If the ball touches you before it hits the ground it must be redropped, and you do not incur a penalty. You can be facing in any direction when dropping the ball.

HAZARDS

GROUND UNDER REPAIR

This is an area where ground maintenance is going on and will be clearly marked, often with a sign stating G.U.R. If your ball is in this area drop it clear at the nearest point of relief without penalty.

CASUAL WATER

If water is visible as you take your stance when playing through the green you are entitled to a free drop. This must be taken at the nearest point which avoids these conditions. It may mean your ball is on the fairway but the nearest point is in the rough - bad luck. Having determined the nearest point of relief drop the ball within one club-length of that point.

BUNKERS

A bunker is an area of bare ground most often a depression, which is usually covered in sand. The grass-covered banks of a bunker are not part of a bunker. Bunkers can be found anywhere on the golf course but mainly they are situated around the green.

When playing a stroke out of a bunker you must not ground the club in the sand when addressing the ball. Neither can you touch the sand in a bunker, or the ground in a hazard before you play a stroke. The penalty for this is two strokes in stroke-play and loss of a hole in match-play. Always rake the bunker after you have played out to ensure the surface is smooth for the next unfortunate player to follow

You must not ground the club into the sand when playing in a bunker.

WATER HAZARDS
It is the duty of the club to define clearly the limits of a water hazard, this is usually done by means of yellow stakes or lines marked on the ground. If you wish you can play your ball as it lies, but you cannot ground your club or touch the hazard during the address or back-swing. The alternative is to drop your ball either under the stroke and distance rule, or for a penalty of one stroke you can drop the ball anywhere behind the hazard, keeping the point where your ball last crossed the line of the hazard between you and the hole.

When dropping the ball make sure you stand so that you are dropping the ball on this line, not to either side.

LATERAL WATER HAZARD
This hazard is water that lies more or less in the direction of the line of play. In most occasions this is a trench for drawing surface water from the fairways. Again the area of the hazard will be clearly defined either with lines on the ground or red stakes.

THE GREEN

Always look after the surface of the green particularly around the hole. Never take your trolley on to the green. Equally if you are carrying your bag of clubs, get

A water hazard at the 10th hole at the Belfry.

Opposite: Always repair your own pitch marks on the green.

into the habit of laying them down off the green. Always repair your own pitch marks.

Never walk on the line of another player's putt; if you are asked to attend the flag, make sure the flag will come out easily before the player putts. When replacing the flag avoid marking the rim of the hole. You can mark your ball, lift it and clean it at anytime on the green. This is done by putting a coin or a ball marker, into or on the surface behind the ball. If your ball is on the line of another player's putt you might be asked to mark it.

Once you are on the green ensure that you either have someone to attend to the flag or that you take it out of the hole. If you hit the flag when putting in match-play you lose one hole, and in stroke-play it counts as a two-stroke penalty. This rule applies even if the flag is out of the hole lying on the green, so be sure it is not in your line. In match-play if your ball is on the green and your ball strikes your opponent's ball, you lose one hole. In stroke-play you are penalized by two strokes and the balls are played as they lie.

WATER ON THE GREEN

If your ball is in casual water on the green you can claim relief and place the ball clear of the water without penalty. This also applies if water on the green is between you and the hole. The ball must be placed at any point that gives relief but not nearer the hole.

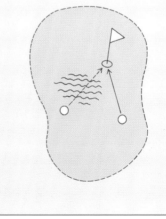

THE WORLD OF
CHAMPIONSHIP
GOLF

ORIGINS AND EARLY DAYS

Most of the world's popular
sports can pinpoint their exact
beginnings, however golf is
not quite sure of its origins.
Realistically, some form of the
game could have been played with
a stick and stone at any point in
history. Early records show that
in 1353 a stick and ball game
was played in Flanders. This
certainly resembled golf as
we know it today.

The Dutch played a similar game called *kolf* which, if not the same as the modern game, certainly sounded like it. Around the same time a stained-glass window was commissioned for Gloucester Cathedral, England depicting a man swinging a stick at a ball. This is the basis of an English claim to being the game's inventors. But the Scots would dispute this. They firmly believe they founded golf because golf's heritage and lore has primarily evolved on the Scottish links.

In Scotland, golf was banned in 1457 by an Act of Parliament as it interfered with archery practice. There were three such edicts. The last was in 1491 by James IV but ten years later he himself took up the game.

The so-called 'Gloucester golfer' window.

Previous page: St Andrews.
Opposite: Golf in Holland.

Left: James IV of Scotland. In 1491 he issued the third edict banning golf.

The Honourable Company of Edinburgh Golfers.

Around sixty years or so later, Mary Queen of Scots gave the game her Royal approval and in the mid-sixteenth century the Archbishop of St Andrews gave his consent for the game to be played in the Burgh. Scotland's claim to be the 'home' of golf is not questioned.

By the eighteenth century, the game had spread throughout Scotland. Organized clubs started to develop. The Edinburgh Golfing Society, later the Royal Burgess Golfing Society of Edinburgh, was formed in 1735 and is the world's oldest golf club. In 1744 the Gentlemen Golfers of Edinburgh, later renamed the Honourable Company of Edinburgh Golfers, were responsible for golf's first set of rules.

167

Golf at Pau in France, by Allen Sealy, 1892.

When the St Andrews Club (later renamed the Royal and Ancient) was formed in 1754, their rules were almost identical to those of the Edinburgh Golfers. But one thing that was not the same was the length of their respective courses: the Edinburgh links had five holes while St Andrews had 22. It was after the latter reduced theirs in 1764 that 18 became the standard number of holes. The growth of golf in Scotland led to the game being taken 'over the border' to England and the first English club dates from 1766 with the formation of the

Royal Blackheath Club.

The first club on continental Europe was founded at Pau in France in 1856 and by the end of the nineteenth century golf had spread to many more parts of the globe. Inevitably the United States would soon fall under the spell of this fast-growing sport. When the St Andrews club in Yonkers, New York, was formed in 1888 with many British members, it helped popularize the game in America. By 1894 the United States Golf

Association was formed, and the greatest golf-playing nation in the world burst into life. In 1860 a competition was organised in Britain to find the champion golfer. And so was born the British Open, which was played over three rounds of Prestwick's 12-hole course and won by Willie Park with a score over 36 holes of 174.

The United States hosted its first Open in 1895 at Newport, Rhode Island, where the winner was Horace Rawlins. Since then major championships, for professionals and amateurs, have developed all over the world.

Golf at Prestwick, Scotland by Michael Brown. The first British Open was played there.

A painting of Victorian ladies playing golf.

Golf being played on the Scheldt, c. 1600.

EVOLUTION AND EQUIPMENT

Golf has come a long way since its beginnings 500 or more years ago. Today it is a multi-million dollar business.

With the constant drive to develop clubs that will hit harder and balls that will fly further, one has to wonder just how the golfing greats of yesteryear would have fared with the modern technology.

THE GOLF BALL

Manufacturers are constantly seeking ways of aiding the golfer. Just as it seems they have developed the 'perfect' golf ball, they come up with another technical advance.

The modern two-piece ball is made of a solid rubber core, encased in a durable dimpled cover, The design and placement of the dimples is all important to the ball's trajectory and flight, therefore, the manufacturers are constantly experimenting with this area.

Golf balls were originally made of wood, and inevitably without the machine tools of today they were not perfectly round. But at the turn of the seventeenth century the wooden ball gave way to the 'feathery', a cased leather ball stuffed with feathers. Again, it was not fully rounded, and because it was hand-made, it lacked uniformity. Nevertheless, it provided extra length

Above: A feathery golf ball, c.1845.

Right: A selection of gutties and rubber core balls.

The modern two-piece ball is made of a solid rubber core, encased in a durable dimpled cover.

and as such was the first development in aiding the golfer with new equipment.

It was not until golf started becoming popular in the mid-nineteenth century that major strides forward were made, when the Reverend Robert Preston invented the 'gutty' ball. The 'gutty' was made of gutta-percha, a glue substance from Malaysia, which could be moulded into a uniform round object.

While the 'gutty' adopted a straight flight when hit correctly, it dropped out of the sky when it came to the end of its trajectory. However, it was soon realized that the 'gutty' travelled further towards the end of a round of golf. This was the result of damage caused to the ball by contact with the clubhead. This led to the development of the dimpled ball, and later the 'Haskell'.

The 'Haskell', so called because it was invented by the American Coburn Haskell, was a three piece, rubber-cored ball, wrapped around with elastic and coated in a dimpled plastic outer-casing. The 'Haskell' with its dimples marked the first resemblance to the golf ball of today.

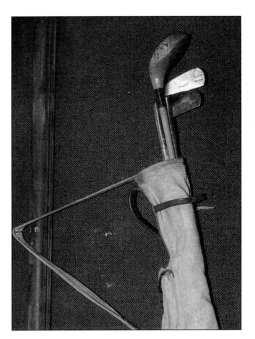

THE GOLF CLUB

Early golf clubs were almost certainly made entirely of wood with the clubhead and shaft being made of different types, glued together and bound in twine. Hazel and ash were used for the shaft, while apple, beech, blackthorn and pear were popular for the head.

Towards the end of the nineteenth century the golf club started to look very different, as an alternative wood, hickory, was used for the club shafts, and iron heads were developed to withstand the battering from the 'gutty', as well as to gain extra distance.

A golf bag and clubs, from the beginning of the twentieth century.

A painting, c. 1600. depicting the use of crude wooden clubs.

172

Old wooden clubs.

While the wooden clubs could meet the demands of the 'gutty', they could not stand up to the 'Haskell' ball, and it was necessary to find a new material for clubheads. The North American wood, persimmon, was discovered to be ideal, but to prevent damage ivory or bone inserts were added to the clubface.

After World War I, hickory was in short supply, and it became necessary to use steel as an alternative material for the club shafts.

Club sets now consisted of 14 clubs, and for the first time, players could buy a complete set of clubs that matched each other in style and design.

Laminated plastic, and then light aluminium, replaced persimmon for use in clubheads, and graphite and titanium shafts were developed to enable more movement of the clubhead through the ball. 'Cavity-back' clubs (irons with the cavity hollowed out of the back of the clubhead) have also been designed to give a more exact centre of gravity.

Modern cavity-back clubs.

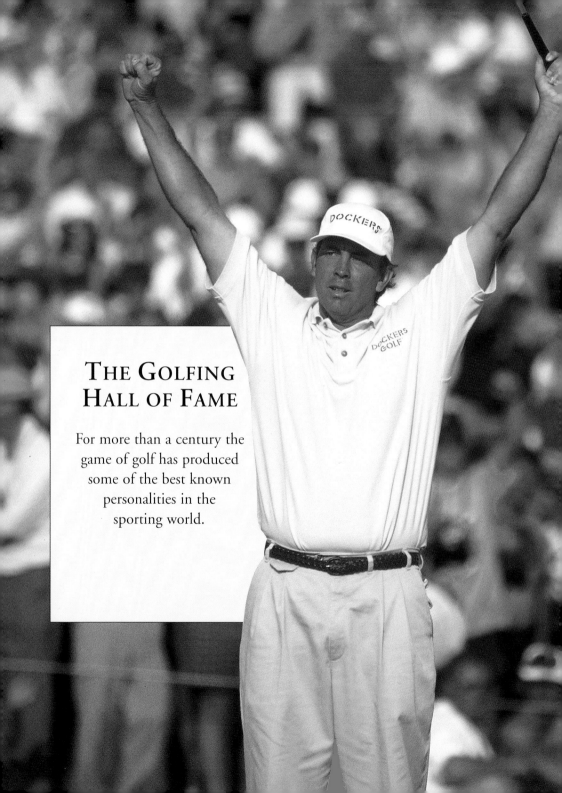

THE GOLFING
HALL OF FAME

For more than a century the
game of golf has produced
some of the best known
personalities in the
sporting world.

ALLAN ROBERTSON

Mid-nineteenth century golfers: Allan Robertson is seventh from the left.

Born St Andrews, Scotland, 1815. Allan Robertson is widely regarded as the first true 'great' of the game of golf. He dominated the sport in the mid-nineteenth century. Following his death, a tournament was organized to find his successor as 'champion' golfer: the British Open Championship.

Robertson had golf in his veins from an early age and he helped run the family golf club and ball manufacturing business that overlooked St Andrews' 18th green. For a while Robertson's assistant was Old Tom Morris. Of the many matches Robertson and Morris played together their most famous victory was against the Dunn brothers, Willie and Jamie. Played over 108 holes at three different links. Morris and Robertson remained unbeaten until Robertson's untimely death at the age of 44, in 1859.

Opposite: Tom Lehman.

TOM MORRIS SENIOR

Born St Andrews, Scotland, 1821. Tom Morris Senior, or 'Old Tom' as he was affectionately known, was one of the first true greats of the game.

After Allan Robertson's death the British Open was inaugurated, in 1860, to find his successor. Many felt the first 'champion' of golf would be Morris, but Willie Park took that honour by two strokes. However, in 1861, Morris beat Park into second place by four strokes. Morris retained his title by 13 strokes, again with Park as runner-up, in 1862. Title number three came in 1864 and in 1867 he became the first man to win four titles.

A painting of Old Tom Morris and Allan Robertson by Thomas Hodge.

His son maintained the family tradition and became the next champion in 1868. Old Tom Morris was head greenkeeper at St Andrews until 1904 when he was aged 83. Remarkably, he played in every British open from 1860 until 1896 and when he captured the title in 1867 he became, and remains, the oldest winner of the championship. He died in 1908.

TOM MORRIS JUNIOR

Born St Andrews, Scotland, 1851. Young Tom Morris won four consecutive British opens in the three years between 1868 and 1870, and again in 1872. There was no championship in 1871 because following his third win Morris was allowed to keep the trophy, the red Moroccan Belt, permanently. In 1872 when the British Open was revived with a new trophy, he became champion again.

He appeared in his first Open at the age of 14 in 1865 and when he captured his first title in 1868 he was only 17; to this day he remains the youngest champion. When he won his third title at 19 in 1870 he lowered the 36-hole championship record by five strokes, and his average of 74.5 strokes per round was not bettered until 1904. His opening round of 47 for Prestwick's 12 holes that year is regarded as one of the truly great rounds of championship golf.

Young Tom finished runner-up to Mungo Park at Musselburgh in 1874. Sadly it was to be the St Andrews man's last Open. Shortly before the 1875 championship, while playing a challenge match at North Berwick, he received a telegram saying both his wife and newborn baby had died. After a bout of heavy drinking and depression Young Tom died on Christmas Day. He was only 24 years of age.

Old and Young Tom Morris, c. 1873.

Young Tom Morris wearing the red Moroccan Open Championship belt in 1870.

JOHN HENRY 'J.H.' TAYLOR

Born Northiam, England, 1871. The only English-born member of the 'Great Triumvirate', John Henry Taylor, known affectionately as 'J.H.' was the son of a Devon labourer. He left school at the age of 11 and after a succession of jobs joined the greenkeeping staff at Westward Ho! Golf Club.

Taylor turned professional at the age of 19 and became greenkeeper at nearby Burnham. Four years later, in 1894, he became the first non-Scottish-born winner of the British Open, when he won by five strokes at Sandwich. He retained the title at St Andrews a year later with an equally convincing four-stroke margin. Title number three came Taylor's way at St Andrews in 1900 which he won by eight strokes from Harry Vardon. Taylor's fourth title was at Deal in 1909. He then won for a fifth time in 1913, achieving victory by eight strokes over Ted Ray.

Taylor was still competing 30 years after his first triumph. Most of Taylor's professional career was spent at the Royal Mid-Surrey Club, and he played a large part in the formation of the Professional Golfer's Association (PGA). He died in 1963.

J.H.Taylor after capturing the 1894 British Open.

Left: A painting of the 'Great Triumvirate', James Braid, Harry Vardon and J.H.Taylor.

HARRY VARDON

Born Jersey, Channel Islands, 1870. Harry Vardon was the most successful of the 'Great Triumvirate' with six British Open titles and one US Open title to his credit. Vardon came to England from Jersey in 1890 and appeared in the British Open three years later. He captured the first record-breaking six titles in 1896. Back-to-back wins came in 1898 and 1899. Vardon then went on to win the US Open at Chicago in 1900.

Vardon won his third British Open in 1903 but had an eight-year wait to win his fifth in 1911. Vardon came close to a second US Open title in 1913 but was beaten in a play-off by the unknown US amateur Francis Ouimet. This was a win that changed the face of golf in America because Ouimet inspired many new golfers. A year later in 1914, Vardon recaptured the British Open at Prestwick. It was Vardon's sixth title. No other player has won so many Open titles. He died in 1937.

Right: Vardon in action in 1900.

Far right: A cigarette card depicting Vardon c. 1912.

HARRY VARDON.
FINISH OF SWING—FULL IRON SHOT.

JAMES BRAID

Born Earlsferry, Scotland, 1870. James Braid was one of the three members of the 'Great Triumvirate' which dominated British golf at the turn of the century, winning 16 British Open titles between them; the other members were Harry Vardon and J.H.Taylor. Braid captured five titles, the first at Muirfield in 1901 when he beat Vardon by three shots. Braid won his second title, at St Andrews in 1905. A four-stroke victory over Taylor ensured Braid retained the title at Muirfield in 1906 and two years later at Prestwick he won his fourth title. His

James Braid on his way to winning his first British Open at Muirfield, in 1901.

score of 291 for the 72 holes remained an Open record until surpassed by the great Bobby Jones in 1927. When Braid won the Open at St Andrews in 1910, he became the first man to win the title five times. Only Harry Vardon has won more British Opens.

James Braid died in 1950 at the age of 80.

A commemorative postcard to celebrate the fiftieth British Open at St Andrews.

TED RAY

Born Jersey, Channel Islands, 1877.
Ted Ray had the misfortune of being
around at the same time as golf's 'Great
Triumvirate'. Nevertheless, he managed
to win the British Open in 1912.

Like Harry Vardon, Ray was born in
Jersey. He first made an impression when
he finished runner-up to James Braid in
the 1901 News of the World tournament. In 1912, Ray won the British
Open when he beat Vardon by four
strokes at Muirfield. The following year
he was beaten into second place by
J.H.Taylor and that same year Ray
finished third in the US Open at
Brookline. But in 1920 Ray became the
first British winner of the US title since
Harry Vardon in 1900, and the oldest
winner at 43 at the Inverness Club, Ohio.

Ray last came close to winning the
British Open in 1925, when he was
runner-up. Two years later he was
honoured with the Ryder Cup captaincy.
He died in 1943.

*Above: Ted Ray, winner of US Open in 1920.
This was the last British win until Jacklin's victory
50 years later.*

*The moment that changed the course of golfing
history. Ouimet on the 18th green with Vardon
and Ray in the US Open at Brookline, 1913.
Ouimet's victory ushered in a period of
American success in championship golf.*

181

WALTER HAGEN

Born Rochester, New York, 1892. Walter Hagen did for professional golf in the 1920's what Arnold Palmer did for sport in the 1960's: he took it to the man in the street and made it the 'people's game'. Both men played a role in dispelling the myth that golf was only for the rich, being down-to-earth men who made people realize that they too could play the game.

Having won the US Open in 1914 and 1919, and the US PGA title in 1921, Hagen captured the British Open at Sandwich in 1922 and became the first American-born winner of the title. After finishing second to Arthur Havers at Troon in 1923 he regained the title in 1924. He followed this Open success by winning the first of four consecutive US PGA titles, in the days when it was played under match-play rules. Back-to-back British Opens followed in 1928 and 1929 as he took his tally of professional Majors to 11, a figure bettered only by Jack Nicklaus. Hagen died at Traverse City, Michigan in 1969 at the age of 76.

The flamboyant Hagen always attracted a large gallery.

Portrait of Hagen by Frank Bensinge, 1957.

Walter Hagen after winning his third British Open title.

GENE SARAZEN

Born Harrison, New York, 1902. Gene Sarazen was involved in two of golf's most talked about incidents, and they came 38 years apart. The first was at Augusta during the final round of the Masters which he won after a play-off against Craig Wood. To get into the play-off, Sarazen holed out a 2-wood from the fairway at the par 5 15th for an albatross (double eagle). It remains one of the most talked-about golf shots in Augusta, Georgia.

The second of Sarazen's memorable shots was at Troon in 1973 when he holed in one at the short 8th Postage Stamp hole in front of millions of television viewers. Sarazen was 71 at the time.

He won both the US Open and US PGA titles in 1922, retained the PGA a year later, and in 1932 he carried off another double when he won the US and British Open titles to become the first professional to win both titles in the same year. He won his third PGA in 1933 and two years later he became the first man to win all four Majors when he won the second Masters titles, thanks to that double-eagle!

Sarazen at the Masters. He was the first man to win all four Majors.

At the 1973 British Open. The day before he had scored an ace.

BOBBY JONES

Born Atlanta, Georgia, 1902. Robert 'Bobby' Tyre Jones never turned professional during his all too brief career, but that did not prevent him from taking on and beating all the top professionals of the 1920's. He rightly earned himself the title of 'greatest amateur golfer of all time'. Jones graduated from college with degrees in law, literature and engineering. He chose law as his profession with golf as his great hobby. He developed one of the finest swings ever seen.

Jones won his first Major in 1923 when he won the US Open after a play-off. The following year he won the first of two successive US Amateur titles. He won both the US and British Open in 1926 and in 1927 he retained his British Open title at St Andrews and made it another double by taking the US Amateur title for the third time. He made it four the

Above: Bobby Jones taking his final drive to win another US Open at Winged Foot, 1929.

Portrait of Bobby Jones by J.A.A. Berrie

following year and in 1929 he maintained his winning streak by capturing the US Open after a 36-hole play-off with Al Espinosa at Winged Foot.

However, the best was still to come because in 1930 Jones first won the British Amateur title at St Andrews, then took the British Open at Hoylake, returned to America to take his fourth US Open and then, on 27 September 1930, completed the game's most remarkable Grand Slam when he added the US Amateur title at Merion. On this triumphant note Bobby Jones decided to retire from competitive golf at the age of 28.

And after he finished playing Jones further ensured his place in the game's hall of fame by giving golf one of its finest courses, the Augusta National, and also the Masters, the great championship which is played there every April. Jones died in his native Georgia on 18 December, 1971.

HENRY COTTON

Born Holmes Chapel, England, 1907. Cotton turned professional at the age of 17 and at 19 was appointed professional at Langley Park. He was a member of the successful British Ryder Cup team of 1929, and in 1947 and 1953 he was honoured with the team's captaincy.

Cotton's domination of European golf started when he captured the Belgian Open in 1930 and it was while he was the professional at Belgium's Waterloo Club that Cotton won his first British Open at Sandwich in 1934; his second-round 65 remained an Open record until bettered by Mark Hayes at Turnberry 43 years later. Cotton won his second Open title at Carnoustie in 1937 and he became the only man to win the title both before and after World War II when he beat defending champion Fred Daly by five strokes at Muirfield in 1948.

During the war Cotton served with the RAF, but was invalided out because of ulcers and a burst appendix. He put his skills to good use by raising money for the Red Cross and was later rewarded with the MBE. Cotton spent much of his retirement in his beloved Portugal before his death in 1987.

Henry Cotton was an inspiration to many golfers in the 1950's.

Henry Cotton proudly holding the trophy after his triumph at Carnoustie.

SAM SNEAD

Born Hot Springs, Virginia, 1912. No man won more events on the US Tour than 'Slammin' Sam Snead. His total of 81 wins between 1936 and 1965 is 11 more than second-place Jack Nicklaus. But remarkably he never won the US Open, the one title he so desperately wanted. He was runner-up on four occasions, including his début in 1937.

Snead's first Tour win was in the 1936 Virginia Closed Championship and his 81st, and last, was in the Greensboro Open - at the age of 52 years and 10 months he became the oldest-ever Tour winner.

SAM SNEAD
PROFESSIONAL GOLF STAR

Sam won seven Majors. His first was in 1942 when he beat Jim Turnesa 2 & 1 to win the US PGA title. Four years later he won the first post-war British Open at St Andrews but his glory years were between 1949 and 1954 when he won the Masters three times and US PGA title twice.

Sam Snead receiving the silver claret jug after winning his first and only British Open. The most successful professional golfer, Snead won 81 US Tour events.

BEN HOGAN

Ben Hogan rightly takes his place as one of the true greats of the game of golf. Born in Texas in 1912, he turned professional in 1931 but had to wait seven years for his first tournament success. But once it came, in the 1938 Hershey Fourball, it was the springboard for greater things. In the 1946 US PGA Championship Hogan captured his first Major and over the next three seasons won 31 tournaments. He regained the US PGA title in 1948 and won the first of four US Open titles. But in 1949 following a bad car accident, Hogan was at first presumed dead but he survived only to be told that he would never play golf again. Eleven months later he took part in the Los Angeles Open and 16 months after his horrific accident he won the fiftieth US Open at Merion. Had the British Open and US PGA Championship not clashed he may well have won all four in one year. To this day no other man has won three Majors in one season.

Ben Hogan, the 1948 US Open Champion.

Hogan after winning the 1953 British Open.

BOBBY LOCKE

Born Germiston, Transvaal, 1917. A former bomber pilot from South Africa, Bobby Locke, dominated the British Open Championship in the late 1940's and 1950's along with Australia's Peter Thomson. They won the title nine times between them.

A professional since 1938, he travelled to Britain after the war. In the first post-war Open, at St Andrews in 1946, he finished runner-up to Sam Snead. Then in America in 1947 he won seven tournaments. The following year he won the Chicago Victory National by a record 16 strokes.

His first British Open title came at Sandwich in 1949, and the following year he beat Argentina's Roberto Vincenzo by two strokes at Troon. Locke beat his great rival Thomson to win his third title at Lytham in 1952 and again when Locke won his fourth open at St Andrews in 1957.

Locke won more than 80 tournaments world-wide, the last being on home soil in the 1958 Transvaal open. A car accident damaged his eyesight in 1960. He died in 1987.

Locke, distinguishable in his white cap.

PETER THOMSON

Born Melbourne, Australia, 1929. In the 1950s, Thomson achieved a twentieth-century record of five British Open titles. His hat trick of wins between 1954 and 1956 had not been achieved since Young Tom Morris 80 years earlier.

Thomson turned professional in 1950 and immediately went on to win his first professional tournament, the New Zealand Open. He won that title nine times and the Australian Open three times; the last being in 1972 at the age of 43.

Two of the top golfers of the 1950s, Locke (left) and Thomson (right).

He first competed in the British Open in 1951 and finished sixth. He lost by one stroke to South Africa's Bobby Locke in 1952, was fourth in 1953, but then won Birkdale's first Open in 1954. He retained his title at St Andrews a year later and completed the hat trick at Hoylake in 1956. He was runner-up to Locke again in 1957, but won again in 1958 when he beat Britain's Dave Thomas in a play-off at Lytham. Just when it looked as though the winning had stopped, Thomson beat the UK pair of Christy O'Connor and Brian Huggett to win at Birkdale for a second time in 1965.

Thomson tried his hand on the US Tour in the 1950s but his long-iron play was not suited to the American courses. However, when he joined the US Seniors' Tour in 1979 his fortunes were reversed and he started winning money on a scale undreamt of in his youth.

Peter Thomson during the 1956 British Open. He went on to win his third title; the first and only hat trick this century.

ARNOLD PALMER

Born Latrobe, Pennsylvania, 1929. Soon after his arrival on the golfing scene in the mid-1950s Arnold Palmer became one of the most popular golfers world-wide. He did what few had done before, and took the game to ordinary people. His enthusiasm for the sport was infectious and he was largely responsible for television and sponsors turning their attention to golf.

Palmer won the US Amateur title in 1954 and turned professional a year later. Before the year was out he had captured the first of his 61 US Tour titles - the Canadian Open, regarded by many as the 'Fifth Major'. The first of his Majors came in 1958 when he won the Masters. Two years later he won both the Masters and US Open. Arnie won the first of two back-to-back British Open titles in 1961,

and played a large part in encouraging his fellow American professionals to make the trip across the Atlantic to the world's greatest golf tournament.

Arnold Palmer never won the US PGA title but added two more Masters titles to his honours when he won in 1962 and 1964. His last victory on the regular US Tour was in 1973 when he won the Bob Hope Desert Classic.

The winning ways returned in 1979 after Arnold Palmer joined the US Seniors Tours.

Left: Arnold Palmer on his way to victory at the British Open, in 1961.

Below: Arnold Palmer and Casper at the 1966 US Open.

GARY PLAYER

At the 1974 British Open.

Born Johannesburg, South Africa, 1935. Gary turned professional at the age of 17 in 1953 and two years later won his first professional title, in Egypt. He made his British début in 1956 and won the Dunlop Tournament at Sunningdale. The first of 21 US Tour event wins, the 1958 Kentucky Derby Open, and a year later he won his first Major when he took the British Open at Muirfield.

Gary Player became the first non-American winner of the Masters in 1961 and a little over 12 months later he also became the first overseas winner of the US PGA title. He completed the 'Grand Slam' of all four Majors in 1965 when he won the US Open. He also won the first of his record five world match-play titles at Wentworth that year. He won the British Open at Carnoustie in 1968 and in 1972 he won a second US PGA title. In 1974 he won his second Masters and then won the British Open at Lytham. Even that great year was later overshadowed by his third Masters success in 1978 when he scored seven birdies in the last ten holes to win the title at the age of 42.

Gary Player continues to enjoy himself on the Seniors Tour.

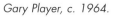

Gary Player, c. 1964.

JACK NICKLAUS

Born Columbus, Ohio, 1940. The potential of Jack Nicklaus was revealed to the American public when he won the 1959 US Amateur title at 19 and then finished second to the great Arnold Palmer in the 1960 US Open. Jack went on to capture his second amateur title in 1961. He turned professional in 1962 and his first win as a paid member of the US Tour was in that year's Open at Oakmont, when he beat Palmer in a play-off. that was to be the first of a record-breaking 18 professional Majors for 'The Golden Bear', as he went on to become the greatest modern-day golfer. He went on to win the US Open on three more occasions, in 1967, 1972 and 1980. He won the US PGA title in 1963, 1971, 1973, 1975 and 1980. He won the British Open on three occasions, 1966, 1970 and 1978.

It was in the Masters at Augusta that Jack enjoyed some of his greatest moments. He won his first Masters in 1963 then had back-to-back wins in 1965 and 1966. After winning in 1972 and 1975 he became the oldest-ever Masters champion at the age of 46 when he recaptured the cherished title in 1986. Jack Nicklaus's 70 regular Tour wins is second only to Sam Snead's all-time

record. Furthermore, Jack has been runner-up on the US Tour an amazing 58 times. In addition, he was top money winner eight times, US PGA player of the Year five times, a member of five Ryder Cup teams, and non-playing captain twice, and appeared on six winning US World Cup teams.

Jack Nicklaus is probably the most successful golfer of all time.

Left: The amateur Jack Nicklaus in 1960.

Jack Nicklaus during the 1977 British Open at Turnberry.

LEE TREVINO

Lee Trevino was born in the Texan city of Dallas to Mexican parents in 1939. From a poor and humble background he went on to be one of the best-loved golfers in the world.

He started caddying at a local course at the age of eight and by the time he was 14 he wanted nothing other than to play golf. Completely self-taught, Trevino turned professional in 1960. His first Tour win was in the US Open at Oak Hill. He went on to win 27 Tour events and represent his country in six Ryder Cup matches. Sadly he was the non-playing captain in 1985 when the United States lost for the first time in 28 years.

Trevino and Mr Lu of Taiwan after they had engaged in a memorable final round in the British Open.

Lee Trevino won the 1971 British Open after a great contest with Mr Lu and Britain's Tony Jacklin. He retained his title at Muirfield a year later, by holing two chips shots and one shot from a bunker, ensuring his victory over Jacklin. His 1971 British Open success was part of a remarkable triple which saw him capture the US, British and Canadian Opens all within 21 days.

He also won the US PGA title twice, in 1974 and 1984.

Lee Trevino has always been one of golf's great characters.

193

TOM WATSON

Born Kansas City, Texas, 1949. Since winning the first of more than 30 US Tour events, the 1974 Western Open, Watson was tipped as the successor to Jack Nicklaus. Their great duel at Turnberry's first British Open in 1977, when he shattered all previous British Open records, was one of the truly memorable clashes in world golf.

The first of Watson's eight Majors was in 1975 when he beat Jack Newton in a play-off at Carnoustie. He completed the Masters/British Open double in 1977 and on both occasions Nicklaus took second place. He won his third British Open at Muirfield in 1980 and when he took his second Masters title in 1981 Nicklaus was the runner-up. Nicklaus was in second place to Watson again in the 1982 US Open at Pebble Beach which Watson won by chipping in from rough just off the green at the 17th on the final day. Watson also won his fourth British Open, at Troon, that year. He equalled Peter Thomson's post-war record a year later in 1983 when he won his fifth open at Birkdale.

In 1989 Watson was one stroke off the lead going into the final round at Troon, but a closing 72 meant he just missed the three-way play-off. But such is his love of the British Open that he will keep trying to achieve that magical sixth win.

Tom Watson taking his fifth British Open title at Birkdale, 1983.

At the British Open, 1977.

SEVERIANO BALLESTEROS

Born Pedrena, Spain, 1957.
Unquestionably the finest golfer produced
by Spain, Seve shot to the forefront of
world golf in 1976 at the British Open
when as a 19-year-old he shared second
place with Jack Nicklaus behind Johnny
Miller at Birkdale. His first Major was in
1979 when he won the British Open at
Lytham with Ben Crenshaw and Jack
Nicklaus sharing second place. He became
the youngest winner of the Masters the

*Seve Ballesteros is the youngest of four brothers
who are all top-quality golfers.*

following year and he regained this title in
1983 with a four-shot victory. He beat
Tom Watson and Bernhard Langer to
capture his second British Open title at
St Andrews in 1984 and his third Open
victory was again at Lytham, in 1988.
A stalwart of the successful European
Ryder Cup team in the 1980s, Seve
became the inspirational captain of the
memorable European win at Valderrama,
Spain in 1997.

*Seve Ballesteros putting during the 1989
Ryder Cup, at the Belfry.*

TOM KITE

Born Austin, Texas, 1949. One of the biggest money winners on the US Tour, Tom Kite became the first man to amass $6 million in prize money in August 1990 when he won the Federal Express St Jude Classic at Memphis. He went on to win over $7 million and in 1992 he eventually threw away the tag of 'being the best golfer never to win a Major' when he captured the US Open at Pebble Beach. He was runner-up in the Masters in 1983 and 1986, and again in the British Open in 1978.

Tom Kite won the US Open in 1992.

A former US Amateur Championship runner-up (he was second to Lanny Wadkins in 1970), Kite represented his country in the Walker Cup before turning professional. He was the PGA's Rookie of the Year in 1973. He has won more than 15 US titles. He has also been honoured with the coveted Bob Jones Award, the PGA Player of the Year title, and was the US captain of the 1997 Ryder Cup team.

At the 1989 Dunhill Cup.

NICK FALDO

Faldo has become one of the world's finest golfers.

won on American soil for the first time in 1984 when he took the Sea Pines Heritage Classic, and in 1987 he captured the British Open at Muirfield. Three years later he won at St Andrews by five shots. In 1992, Faldo went on to win a third British Open title, the first Briton to do so since Henry Cotton.

He has also won the US Masters three times: back-to-back titles in 1989 and 1990, followed by his third win in 1996.

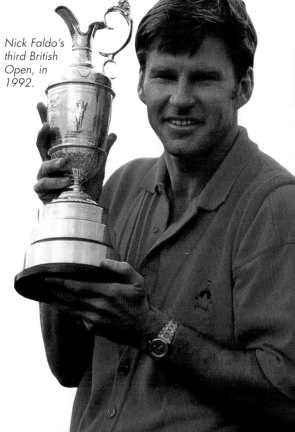

Nick Faldo's third British Open, in 1992.

Born Welwyn Garden City, England, 1957. Nick Faldo emerged as a potential champion in 1975 when he captured the English Amateur title at the age of 18 and two years later he was the youngest member of the British Ryder cup team. Rookie of the year in 1977, he went on to win the PGA title three times between 1978 and 1981.

However, Faldo was still keen to improve and at the end of the 1983 season went to coach David Leadbetter to rebuild his swing. His record since then shows the decision was fully justified. He

BERNHARD LANGER

Born Anhausen, Germany, 1957. In the 1980s, Langer vied with Severiano Ballesteros as the leading European golfer and in 1981 and 1984 he toppled the Spaniard from the top of the European money-list. Since winning his first major title, the Cacharel Under-25s Championship by 17 strokes in 1979, he has been one of the top money winners in Europe, winning over 30 tournaments worldwide.

Bernhard enjoyed one of his proudest moments in golf in 1981 when he became the first German to win the German Open. That same year he finished second to Bill Rogers in the British Open and he was runner-up, to Ballesteros, in 1984.

Bernhard Langer during the Ryder Cup, 1989.

Langer has twice been Masters champion at Augusta. In 1985 he came from six behind at the half-way stage to take the title from Ballesteros, Curtis Strange and Raymond Floyd after two brilliant rounds of 68. Eight years later in 1993 Langer had his second Masters victory winning by four shots.

One of Europe's leading golfers.

GREG NORMAN

Born Queensland, Australia, 1955. Greg Norman turned professional in 1976 and then joined the European Tour. In 1977 he won the Martini International. In 1982 Norman was top money winner in Europe after winning the Dunlop Masters, Benson & Hedges Masters, and State Express Classic. But he had to wait until 1984 for his first US Tour win when he won the Kemper and Canadian Opens.

In 1986, his finest year, he was top money winner in America and second highest in Europe. He captured his first Major when a brilliant second round 63 in the British Open contributed to his five stroke win at Turnberry. Norman came close to becoming the first man to win all four Majors in one year: a brilliant final round 65 by Jack Nicklaus prevented victory in the Masters, and in the US Open at Shinnecock Hills, Norman shot a final round 75 which gave the title to Ray Floyd. In the US PGA Championship, Norman again led going into the final round but lost out, to a surprise winner, Bob Tway, who chipped into the hole from a bunker at the 18th.

Norman has never been out of the top 10 of world ranked golfers since 1986 and was ranked number 1 at the end of 1995. He has lost play-offs in all four Majors, but was at his stunning best against Nick Faldo and Corey Pavin at the 1993 British Open at Royal St George's scoring a final round 64 and winning by two strokes.

During the US PGA, 1994 at Southern Hills.

One of the real characters of the modern game.

THE GREAT WOMEN GOLFERS

While it is only in more modern
times that the ladies' professional
game has flourished, women have
been playing competitive golf as
long as their male counterparts.
In Babe Zaharias, the world of
sport not only saw one of the
finest lady golfers of all-time,
but one of the world's great
all-round athletes.

MILDRED ZAHARIAS

Born Port Arthur, Texas, 1914. Mildred Didrikson was known affectionately as 'Babe' because of her adoration for baseball legend Babe Ruth. Mildred won national honours as a basketball player but before the 1932 Olympics she competed in the National Track and Field Championships. She won six of the eight events she entered and set three world records.

Mildred was selected for the Olympics but was only allowed to enter three events. She won two of her three, with record breaking performances in the hurdles and javelin. Although disqualified in the high jump she was allowed to keep her share of the world record.

After the Olympics, Mildred turned her attention to her next sport - golf, typically she became an outstanding competitor. From 1946 to 1947 she won 14 straight tournaments, and in 1947 was the first US winner if the British Amateur Championship. She turned professional the next year and won the US Women's Open, and was top money winner of the US Ladies' Tour for 1948 -51. She won a second Open by nine strokes in 1950.

In 1953 Mildred had surgery for cancer, but 18 months later captured the US Women's Open for a third time. The girl voted 'Athlete of the Half Century' lost her battle with cancer and died in 1956.

Zaharias with the 1954 US Open trophy.

Zaharias at the 1932 Olympics.

Opposite: Laura Davies.

MICKEY WRIGHT

Born San Diego, California, 1935.
Mickey Wright stands second only to
Kathy Whitworth as the most successful
lady golfer in the US. Her total of 82
Tour wins is just six behind Whitworth's
tally.

In the 1960s Wright was invincible,
becoming the top money winner, by winning 44 tournaments between 1961 and
1964. In 1963 she won a record 13 tournaments in a season. She notched up 12
women's Majors winning the US Women's
Open four times, the first in 1958 aged
23 and later that year did the double winning the US LPGA Championship.
Mickey twice won both the Western
Open and Titleholders Championship,
neither of which
exist today.

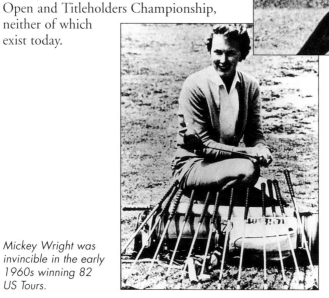

Mickey Wright, one
of the most successful
woman golfers of all
time.

Mickey Wright was
invincible in the early
1960s winning 82
US Tours.

KATHY WHITWORTH

Born Monahans, Texas, 1939, Kathy Whitworth has been to the ladies' game what Sam Snead was to the men's game, both winning more tournaments than any other professional. Kathys' tally of 88 is seven better than 'Slammin' Sam's but neither won their respective US Open titles. The nearest Kathy came was in 1971 when she finished second to JoAnne Carner.

Between 1965 and 1973 she was top money winner eight times in nine years, when she won 61 of her 88 tournaments. Of her six Majors, the first was the 1965 Titleholders Championship. In 1982 she reached the record of the most women's titles and the following year became the first woman to win $1million.

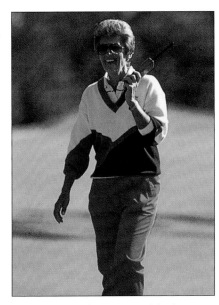

Kathy Whitworth was one of the best putters in the ladies game.

Kathy Whitworth with Karsten Solheim at the 1990 Solheim Cup.

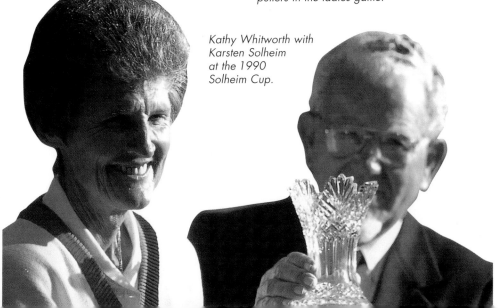

PAT BRADLEY

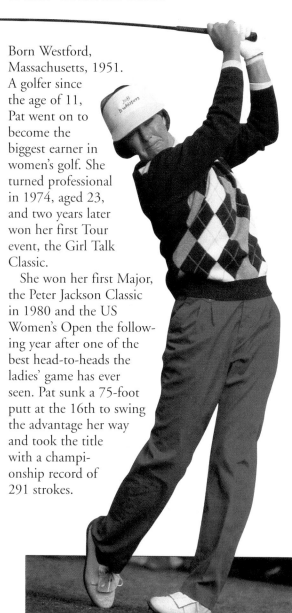

Born Westford, Massachusetts, 1951. A golfer since the age of 11, Pat went on to become the biggest earner in women's golf. She turned professional in 1974, aged 23, and two years later won her first Tour event, the Girl Talk Classic.

She won her first Major, the Peter Jackson Classic in 1980 and the US Women's Open the following year after one of the best head-to-heads the ladies' game has ever seen. Pat sunk a 75-foot putt at the 16th to swing the advantage her way and took the title with a championship record of 291 strokes.

Pat Bradley at the 1990 Solheim Cup, Lake Nona.

She has won six Majors, the US LPGA, Nabisco Dinah Shore and Du Maurier, all in 1986. This was a memorable year when she took home nearly $½ million, from winning five tournaments and became the first person to surpass $2 million in winnings. She is the most successful lady golfer of all time, taking her earnings to $4.3 million.

Pat Bradley.

AMY ALCOTT

Born Kansas City, Texas, 1956. Amy won her first Tour as a professional in 1975, capturing the Orange Blossom Classic aged 19. Consistently winning has been her trade mark and she has amassed more than $3 million in prize-money, winning more than 30 events.

Alcott won her first Major, the Peter Jackson Classic (now the Du Maurier

Above: Amy Alcott after winning the 1988 Nabisco Dinah Shore Classic.

Classic) in 1979 and in 1980 won the US Women's Open with a four-round record total of 280 and took the first $20,000 cheque in US Open history. She also won the Nabisco Dinah Shore three times, in 1983, 1988 and 1991.

Away from golf, Amy Alcott also devotes her time raising money for sufferers of Multiple Sclerosis.

LAURA DAVIES

Born Coventry, England, 1963.
Laura Davies can probably claim to be the greatest British woman golfer of all time and since 1994 has been the world's leading woman golfer. In 1996, she was ranked number 1 on the Ping Leaderboard winning nine of the 31 tournaments she entered including two majors in six different countries. She had eight

Above: Laura Davies the world's leading woman golfer.

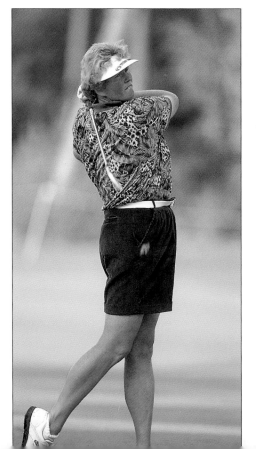

top five finishes and her worldwide earnings exceeded £1million.

Previously, Laura had won the British Women's Open in1986 followed by the US Women's Open in 1987.

Other career highlights include a new world record-breaking 25 under par at the 1995 Irish Open, and her fourth appearance for Europe against the USA in the 1996 Solheim Cup.

Left: At 5'10", Laura Davies is a powerful hitter.

Opposite : Colin Montgomerie at the Masters.

THE GREAT TOURNAMENTS

Although golf matches and tournaments have been played for more than 200 years, championship golf as we know it today started in October 1860 with the first British Open at Prestwick, in Scotland. Since that memorable day, many more championships have been inaugurated.

THE MAJORS

The British Open, US Open, US Professional Golfers Championship (US PGA) and the Masters are the four major championships which are played each year. Although they are collectively referred to as the Grand Slam, no one has ever won all the titles in the same year, and only four players - Gene Sarazen, Ben Hogan, Jack Nicklaus and Gary Player - have won them all.

A painting of the Open championship at St Andrews by Michael Brown.

THE BRITISH OPEN

It all started on Wednesday 17 October 1860 when eight top golfers gathered at Scotland's Prestwick links to play three rounds of the 12-hole course. All entrants, with the exception of George Brown from Blackheath, London, were members of Scottish clubs. The first Open champion was Musselburgh's Willie Park, with a

winning score of 174 for the 36 holes. Old Tom Morris won the second title and became the first great champion, winning the Open four times between 1861 and 1867. He was succeeded by his son, Young Tommy, who won four successive titles between 1868 and 1872. There was no tournament in 1871 because Young Tom was allowed to keep the trophy, the red Moroccan belt, after his third successive win in 1870. When he won his fourth title, he was presented with the silver claret jug which remains one of the most cherished trophies in world golf. Sadly, Young Tom Morris died at an early age but there were plenty of aspirants ready to challenge for the game's senior trophy, and Jamie Anderson (1877-79) and Bob Ferguson (1880-82) both won three successive titles. It would be 70 years before that feat was emulated.

Prestwick staged each of the first 12

Left: Willie Park Senior just after he had won the first British Open, 1860.

Walter Hagen recovers from the sand in the 1929 British Open.

championships, but by the turn of the century, St Andrews, Musselburgh, Muirfield, Sandwich and Hoylake had all hosted the championship. Along with the new courses came new champions, but the success of Taylor at Sandwich in 1894 heralded the start of an era in Open Championship golf.

One of the 'Great Triumvirate', along with James Braid and Harry Vardon, Taylor and his colleagues dominated the event and won it 16 times between them in the 21 years from 1894 to 1914.

After World War I the Americans had their first breakthrough when Jock Hutchison, an exiled Briton, took the trophy across the Atlantic for the first time in 1921. A year later the flamboyant

Hagen became the first American-born winner. The British domination was over and, apart from the occasional victory, they have never really regained it.

With the arrival of amateur Bobby Jones, British fans were privileged to witness one of the finest golfers ever seen, amateur or professional. He won the Open in 1926 and 1927 and in 1930 he beat American professionals Leo Diegel and Macdonald Smith by two strokes to capture his third title.

Britons regained their domination in the latter half of the 1930s with the first of Henry Cotton's three triumphs in 1934. It looked as though the swing would return to the Americans after Sam Snead won at St Andrews in 1946 but victories for Fred Daly and Henry Cotton, brought about renewed optimism

Arnold Palmer, 1961.

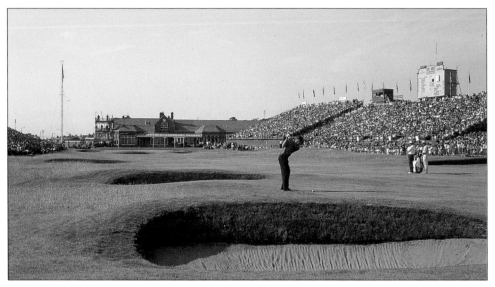

for the British. But it was short-lived because the next 12 years saw the British Open dominated by South Africa's Bobby Locke and Australia's Peter Thomson sharing nine titles between them.

By the end of the 1950s, the number of American professionals making the journey across the Atlantic each year was gradually declining. But Arnold Palmer changed all that. He came to Royal Birkdale in 1961, and carried off the title. He retained it at Troon a year later, but more importantly, he made sure his fellow Americans made the annual trip, thus preventing the Open from losing its status as the world's top tournament.

Palmer's arrival also heralded the start of golf's next 'Triumvirate' - Palmer, Jack Nicklaus and Gary Player. They won the Open eight times between them. American golfers once again started to

Justin Leonard on his way to winning the 1997 British Open at Troon, Scotland.

Seve Ballesteros in 1979 when he captured his first Open title.

dominate the event in the 1960s though Tony Jacklin became the first home champion for 18 years, at Royal Lytham and St Anne's in 1969.

This was Britian's last win until Sandy Lyle's triumph at Sandwich 16 years later. In the meantime, America's Tom Watson had won his first title at Carnoustie in 1975. That was the first of his five wins including his remarkable triumph by one stroke over Jack Nicklaus at Turnberry in 1977.

In 1979 Severiano Ballesteros won the first of three titles at Lytham. Ballesteros won the title for a second time in 1984 bringing about the end of the American supremacy. Since then the trophy has only once gone to America, when Mark Calcavecchia was the surprise winner at Troon in 1989.

The 1980s and early 1990s really belonged to Britian. Sandy Lyle started this winning streak at Sandwich in 1985,

American Tom Lehman captured the British Open at Royal Lytham in 1996.

Below: In 1985 Sandy Lyle became the first British winner of the Open since Tony Jacklin.

and then Nick Faldo won three titles, in 1987, 1990 and 1992, to become the first Briton since Henry Cotton to achieve a hat trick of wins.

Australia too had had a return to those glory days of the 1950s with Greg Norman winning twice in 1986 and 1993 and Ian Baker-Finch in 1991. Nick Price of South Africa won in 1994. Since then Americans have been intent on adding their names to the world's best-known golfing trophy: John Daly 1995, Tom Lehman 1996, Justin Leonard 1997.

THE US OPEN

After the British Open the US Open is the second oldest of the four Majors, having been first played at Newport, Rhode Island, on 4 October 1895. The winner was English-born Horace Rawlins with a score of 173. In 1900 Britain's leading player, Harry Vardon, captured the title and helped popularize the game in America. He did what Palmer did for the British Open in the 1960s.

Johnny McDermott became the first American-born winner in 1911, retaining his title the following year. When Francis Ouimet, won at Brookline in 1913 he beat Vardon and Ted Ray, in a three-way play-off, and confirmed the end of British domination. Tony Jackin's win at Hazeltine in 1970 has been the only British success since then.

Above: Still in discomfort from his accident the previous year, Ben Hogan miraculously went on to win the US Open in 1950.

Most of the great names of American golf have won the US Open. Bobby Jones, Ben Hogan, Willie Anderson and Jack Nicklaus have all won it a record four times. Walter Hagen won the Open at only his second attempt in 1914. Hagen's great rival of the 1920s, Gene Sarazen, took his first Major in 1922 when he won the Open at Skokie, Illinois.

Left: Francis Ouimet, the surprise winner of the 1913 US Open. His victory changed the shape of world golf.

Johnny Miller, Andy North, Hale Irwin, Jerry Pate and Hubert Gree, Larry Nelson, Fuzzy Zoeller and Curtis Strange all won the title in the 1970s and 1980s. Tom Kite won in 1992 followed by Lee Janzen 1993, Ernie Els 1994, Corey Pavin 1995 and Steve Jones 1996.

In 1997, South African Ernie Els became champion for the second time defeating Scotland's Colin Montgomerie. Montgomerie's defeat reminds us that, since Jacklin's success in 1970 and apart from Els, the only non-American winner has been Australia's David Graham in 1981.

The Open has seen many great moments but for sheer brilliance Ben Hogan's triumph at Merion in 1950 will never be surpassed. Having survived a head-on car crash in 1949, he made a remarkable comeback and defied all medical advice to take his second Open championship just 18 months later.

Tony Jacklin became the first British winner of t he US Open for 50 years at Hazeltine in 1970.

At the end of 72 holes Hogan was tied with George Fazio and Lloyd Mangrum on 287. An 18 hole play-off was required and Hogan beat the other two, and many sceptics, by four and six strokes respectively for a tremendous, and emotional, win.

For the up and downs of the Open, Arnold Palmer will probably not need reminding about how he threw away the 1966 Championship at the Olympic Club, California. After three rounds Palmer led Billy Casper by three strokes. With nine holes left he had increased his lead to seven strokes. Victory seemed assured - but nothing is certain in golf until the last putt is sunk. Casper gained shots at the 10th and 13th, but Palmer met with disaster at the par 3 15th after he two-putted for a four while Casper made a birdie. Suddenly the lead was cut to one after the next hole when Casper made a birdie four to Palmer's bogey six at the 604-yard par 5 after a wayward shot.

A five to Casper's par 4 at 17 meant they were all square going into the 18th. Both men made par at the last and so a play-off was required. Palmer trailed by

Arnold Palmer (left) and Jack Nicklaus (right). During the 1967 US Open.

two after nine holes and ran out losing four shots. It is stories such as this which help make tournaments like the US Open as great as they are.

THE MASTERS

The Masters is one of the most coveted prizes in golf despite the fact that it is the youngest of the four Majors. The Masters and the Augusta National course over which it is played were both the brainchild of Augusta-born Bobby Jones, one of the greatest amateur golfers of all time. The first Masters in 1934 did not arouse the interest Jones had hoped, and in an effort to attract media attention he came out of retirement. Horton Smith was the winner by one stroke from Craig Wood.

The following year Wood was runner-up again, after losing a play-off to Gene Sarazen. Sarazen was trailing Wood by three strokes when he came to the par 5 15th in the final round. After a good drive, he took a 4-wood and holed his shot from 220 yards for an albatross (double eagle) two. Three pars then assured him of a play-off and ultimate victory.

Ben Hogan and Sam Snead dominated the event in the early post-war years, winning five titles in six years between 1949 and 1954. They were followed by Arnold Palmer and Jack Nicklaus who between them dominated the event in the late 1950s and 1960s.

Horton Smith, winner of the first Masters in 1934.

A collection of official Masters badges.

Nicklaus seemed to make the Masters his own event, recording six wins. Nicklaus first won by one stroke from Tony Lema in 1963 but his second title in 1965 was by nine strokes from his great rivals Palmer and Gary Player. He became the first man to win back-to-back titles in 1966. Triumph number four was in 1972, and in 1975 he held off a challenge from Johnny Miller and Tom Weiskopf to win his fifth.

European golfers have recently been more successful in the Masters. Severiano Ballesteros became champion in 1980 and 1983. In 1985 Germany's Bernhard Langer also took the trophy to Europe. Then Sandy Lyle became the first British champion in 1988.

Nick Faldo won back-to-back titles in 1989 and 1990. Ian Woosnam won in 1991 to make it four successive wins for British Golfers. In 1992, Fred Couples,

took the trophy back 'home'.But it was in European hands again in 1993 when Bernhard Langer won his second Masters and in 1994 when the Spaniard Jose-Maria Olazabel won. The trophy returned to America when Ben Crenshaw won in 1995. Faldo won his third title in 1996, then Tiger Woods became the youngest ever winner at 21 in 1997.

Right: Ian Woosnam, 1991.
Below: Tiger Woods went on to win in 1997.

UNITED STATES PGA CHAMPIONSHIP

Although it is one of golf's four Majors, the US PGA Championship receives less publicity world-wide than the other three, largely because entry is based on performances in the United States. Consequently there have been fewer non-American winners, among them Gary Player of South Africa in 1962 and 1972, the Australian pair, David Graham and Wayne Grady, in 1979 and 1990, and another South African, Nick Price has won twice in 1992 and 1994.

Traditionally the last of the four Majors each year, the first PGA Championship was held at Siwanoy, New York, in 1916. Jim Barnes, an Englishman living in America, won the final by one hole. The event was played under match-play conditions until 1958.

It was during its match-play days that the Championship brought out the best in Walter Hagen, who won five titles in seven years between 1921 and 1927.

Jack Nicklaus has since equalled Hagen's record of five wins. Gene Sarazen and Sam Snead have three wins each,

In the match-play days, the greatest final was in 1930 when the American Tommy Armour beat Gene Sarazen. On the last Tommy Armour holed a putt from 14 feet. Gene Sarazen then played a similar putt to stay level but missed by inches and thus threw away the chance of his third title.

English-born Jim Barnes (putting) was the first US PGA champion in 1916, beating Scottish-born Jock Hutchison by one hole.

Below: South African-born Nick Price won his first US PGA at Bellerive in 1992. His second win in 1994 was at Southern Hills,

THE TEAM TOURNAMENTS

THE RYDER CUP

When it comes to team tournaments there is none greater than the Ryder Cup, a biennial match between professional golfers from the United States and Europe.

It is named after a British seed merchant, Samuel Ryder. In the late nineteenth century, after overwork brought about a decline in Ryder's health, he joined the local Verulam Golf Club, at St Albans. Suddenly, golf became the new 'love' of his life.

He was captain of the club three times and he enticed many of the leading professionals of the day to compete in tournaments at the Verulam, including the 'Great Triumvirate' of Braid, Taylor and Vardon. A great friend of Ryder's was professional Abe Mitchell, and it was probably at his suggestion that Ryder set up the Ryder Cup. The golfer depicted on the lid of the Ryder Cup trophy is modelled on Mitchell. The idea for a regular match came after the professionals of Britain and the United States met in a match at Wentworth in 1926; the British team won by 13½ - 1½.

Twelve months later, on 3 and 4 June 1927, two eight-man teams from America and Great Britain met at Worcester, Massachusetts, with Walter Hagen and Ted Ray as the respective captains of the first official Ryder Cup teams.

Above: Samuel Ryder (right) with his good friend Abe Mitchell. It is said that the statue on top of the Ryder Cup is modelled on Mitchell.

Programmes from the two Ryder Cup matches played at the Southport and Ainsdale links in Lancashire, England. Britain won in 1933.

America won the first match 9 ½ - 2 ½, but two years later when it was held on British soil, at Moortown , Leeds, Britain gained revenge when George Duncan led the British team to victory by 7-5. The Americans won on home soil again two years later and Britain levelled the series at 2-all after a narrow 6 ½ - 5 ½ win at Southport and Ainsdale in 1933. But that was to be Britain's last success for 24 years as the Americans dominated Sam Ryder's tournament.

The trophy went across the Atlantic in the two remaining pre-war tournaments and when it was revived at Pinehurst in 1947 it was a repeat performance with the Americans winning 11-1. It was closer at Ganton two years later, but it was not until 1957 that the team from Great Britain, led by Dai Rees, recaptured the title at Lindrick, near Sheffield. But that was to be the last time for 28 years that a British team would win the Ryder Cup because the Americans took command. In 1979 to make the contest closer' players from

Above: Sam Snead served his country in nine Ryder Cup matches.

Dai Rees (front centre) with the British team.

Captain Seve Ballesteros and his victorious European team of 1997 in Valderrama, Spain.

Europe became eligible for selection. Spaniards Antonio Garrido and Severiano Ballesteros became the first players from other European countries to join the British team which opposed the Americans at Greenbrier, West Virginia, in 1979. Their presence did little to change matters and the Americans won 17-11. It was similar story at Walton Heath, Surrey, in 1981. However, after the appointment of Tony Jacklin in 1983 as Europe's captain, at the PGA National in Florida, Europe pushed the hosts all the way before losing by one point. Two years later in 1985 on 'home' soil at The Belfry, the Europeans inflicted the first defeat on the Americans since 1957.

That was not only the start of a great run of success for the European team, it was also the start of great media coverage which the Ryder Cup had never received before.

In 1987 Jacklin's men made more history when they travelled to Jack Nicklaus's Muirfield Village Course at Columbus, Ohio, and came away as the first team to

beat the Americans on home soil. Ironically, the American team was skippered by Nicklaus.

Europe retained the trophy after a 14-14 draw at The Belfry in 1989 but the trophy reverted to American hands in 1991 and 1993. However in 1995 the Europeans had a dramatic win at Oak Hill. Then in 1997, Seve Ballesteros' team retained the Cup for Europe by one point in a nerve wracking 14½ to 13½ finish.

The Ryder Cup is now always eagerly awaited as Sam Ryder's trophy has become the top international team event in world golf.

THE WALKER CUP

The Walker Cup is the amateur's equivalent of the Ryder Cup, and it predates its professional counterpart by five years. The idea of an international team tournament, was first put forward in 1920 by Herbert Walker, President of the United States Golf Association. In 1921 a challenge match between America and Britain was played for the International Challenge Trophy. The local press dubbed it the 'Walker Cup'. This was the first unofficial match and the United States won 9-3. The first official Walker Cup was played a year later at Long Island, New York, and the Americans won again, this time 8-4. It was contested annually until 1924, but it then became a biennial event.

The British team suffered some heavy defeats prior to World War II. They were trounced 11-1 at Chicago in 1928 and 10-2 at Sandwich two years later. They did not enjoy their first win until 1938, when they won 7½ - 4½ at St Andrews.

In post-war years the Americans won the Ryder Cup every two years, until a draw in 1965 gave some hope to the British team. Britain's second victory did not come until 1971 when Michael Bonallack led the team to a great 13-11 win at St Andrews. In 1989, the British team captured the trophy for the third time, and the first on American soil, with a one-point win in a close contest at Peachtree, Georgia. The US regained the trophy in 1991 and retained it in 1993. The British team had an exciting win at Royal Porthcawl in 1995, only for the US to win again at Quaker Ridge in 1997.

US Walker Cup victory in 1997.

THE CURTIS CUP

The ladies' equivalent of the Walker Cup is the Curtis Cup, named after sisters Harriot and Margaret Curtis who represented the United States in an international match against Great Britain at Cromer, Norfolk, in 1905; Britain won 6-1.

After several years of unofficial matches the Curtis sisters donated a trophy for a biennial match between the two countries. In 1932, the first match was played at Wentworth, Surrey and was won by the United States 5½-3½.

The Curtis sisters, Harriot (left) and Margaret (right), were talented golfers in their own right.

America won at Chevy Chase two years later but Britain managed a draw at Gleneagles in 1936 when Jessie Anderson holed a 20 foot putt on the last green to win her match and force a tie. It was a memorable moment.

The British team enjoyed success, at Muirfield in 1952 and Sandwich in 1956, and they forced a great draw at Brae Burn, Massachusetts, in 1958. But that was the end of the British success for nearly 30 years until enjoying back-to-back wins at Prairie Dunes, Kansas, in 1986 and at Sandwich two years later. The American women

The moment of victory for the British team at Hoylake in 1992.

regained the trophy with a vengeance at New Jersey in 1990 with a convincing 14-4 win, but the British team re-stamped their authority with a 10-8 win at Hoylake in 1992. Britain and Ireland retained the 1994 trophy with a draw. Then were clear winners again in 1996 at Killarney.

THE EISENHOWER TROPHY

First held in 1958, the Eisenhower Trophy is similar in conception to the idea first put forward by George Walker back in 1920. It is an international team competition for teams of four players. The trophy is named after the former US President, Dwight D. Eisenhower, who was himself a keen golfer.

The first Eisenhower Trophy was contested at St Andrews in October 1958 and won by Australia who beat the Unites States in a play-off. The individual prize for the lowest aggregate score was shared by Bruce Devlin (Australia), Reid Jack (Scotland) and Bill Hyndman

American President Dwight D. Eisenhower (left) seen here with Arnold Palmer.

(USA). The winner of the second individual title at Merion two years later was Jack Nicklaus, who was also a member of the winning American team.

America, Australia and Great Britain and Ireland won the first 13 competitions between them, but the 1980s saw breakthroughs by teams from other countries such as Japan and Canada. There were also first time victories for the Swedish team in 1990 and the New Zealand team in 1992. The Americans do however still hold the record of nine wins in this event.

Scott Hoch at the US PGA in 1997, has been a consistent winner on the US Tour.

AMATEUR CHAMPIONSHIPS

THE BRITISH AMATEUR CHAMPIONSHIP

In 1885, Thomas Owen Potter of Hoylake organized a competition over his home links at Royal Liverpool to find the champion amateur golfer of Britain. Allan McFie, a Scottish member of the host club, beat Horace Hutchinson 7&6 in the final.

The following year the championship gained recognition by the Royal and Ancient who took over the organization of the event and the second championship was won by the inaugural year's runner-up, Hutchinson.

It has been a match-play competition since its formation, but in the 1980s a medal competition was introduced to reduce the field to 64 before changing to match-play conditions.

John Ball, himself a member of the Royal Liverpool Club, won the title a record eight times between 1888 and 1912 and is one of three men, along with Harold Hilton and Bobby Jones, to win both the British Amateur and British Open titles. The biggest winning margin in any final was achieved by America's Lawson Little who beat Britain's Jack Wallace 14&13 in the 1934 final at Prestwick.

John Ball bunkered. Ball, won the British Amateur Championship a record eight times.

Jose-Maria Olazabal was British Amateur Champion in 1984.

The same year, Little won the US Amateur title by 8&7.

Some famous golfers have won the trophy over the years but only one has managed to win it three years in succession, Michael Bonallack, between 1968 and 1970. Deane Beman, commissioner of the US PGA Tour, was the 1959 winner and in recent years the best-known winner has been Spain's Jose-Maria Olazabal, who took the title in 1984.

THE UNITES STATES AMATEUR CHAMPIONSHIP

Following a number of unofficial championships this tournament was officially launched in 1895, ten years after its British counterpart.

It was first played at Newport, Rhode Island, over the same course and in the same week as the inaugural US Open. The first champion was Charles Macdonald from Chicago who beat C.E. Sands 12&11.

All championships up to 1965 were under match-play conditions. From 1965 to 1972 it was a stroke-play event but it reverted to match-play in 1973.

The legendary Bobby Jones won a record five titles in the seven years between 1924 and 1930, his Grand Slam year.

Post-war winners of the title have included some notable names who went on to make their mark in the professional game in the United States. The 1953 champion was Gene Littler and a year later Arnold Palmer was the Amateur Champion. Jack Nicklaus won the title twice, in 1959 and 1961, and in more recent times Lanny Wadkins, Craig Stadler, Jerry Pate, John Cook and Mark O'Meara have all gone from being Amateur Champion to make successful professional careers.

Tiger Woods was US Amateur Champion in 1994, 1995 and 1996, before becoming a professional.

THE WOMEN'S MAJORS

THE US WOMEN'S OPEN
Like the men, ladies' professional golf currently has four Majors, the oldest of which is the US Women's Open, which was launched in 1946. The first champion was Patty Berg. In the final she beat Betty Jameson in the only match-play tournament. All subsequent Opens have been under medal conditions. Betsy Rawls and Mickey Wright have each won the title a record four times. Swedish golfer Annika Sorenstam won back-to-back titles in 1995 and 1996

THE LPGA CHAMPIONSHIP
The Championship was inaugurated in 1955, five years after the formation of the US LPGA, and was won by Beverly Hanson. Like the Open, it started life as a match-play event before becoming a medal event only one year later.

Mickey Wright has been the most successful golfer in this championship, as well as the Open, with four wins. Britain's Laura Davies won in 1994.

THE DU MAURIER CLASSIC.
This was granted Major status in 1979, having been launched in 1973 as La Canadienne, and between 1974 and 1982 it was known as the Peter Jackson Classic, before becoming The Du Maurier in 1983. The first winner was Amy Alcott in 1979, but the most successful player has been Pat Bradley with three wins.

THE NABISCO DINAH SHORE
One of the Majors since 1983, this event was originally set up in 1972 when it was known as the Colgate-Dinah Shore. The change to its present name coincided with it being granted Major status. Amy Alcott was the first winner in 1983 and she has won the event a record three times.

Left: Mickey Wright, had 82 wins on the US Tour.

Right: Patty Sheehan in 1992 when she won the US Open.

THE GOLFING TOURS

Competitive golf for professional players, both male and female, is available weekly throughout the year and is possible in all parts of the globe, thanks to the various tours organized by the different golfing bodies.

THE US PGA TOUR
Originally, this tour was started in 1899 when the Western Open was added to the American golfing calendar to make it, along with the US Open, a two-event tour. But it was not until after the formation of the US PGA in 1916 that a tour as it is known today got under way.

It started in the 1920s when club professionals, with little work in the winter months, would gather in the warmer southern states, starting in the West and moving to the East coast before returning to their summer jobs in the clubs.

When the likes of Walter Hagen, Gene Sarazen and the amateur Bobby Jones joined the 'Tour' it gained in popularity and aided the establishment of such events as the Texas Open and the Los Angeles Open, which have remained high points of the Tour and have helped the game develop as a spectator sport.

After the war the US PGA became more of a national tour, organization improved, and when television showed an interest, prize-money increased. The effect of this is evident today as the US PGA Tour is now one of the most prestigious tours in the world.

In 1968 the professionals took control when they formed the Tournament Players' Division, and since then the Tour has gone from strength to strength, with prize-money exceeding $50 million per season, and the top money winner pocketing over $1million.

THE VOLVO TOUR
The European PGA Tour, now know as the Volvo Tour following a corporate sponsorship deal with the Swedish car

Corporate sponsorship and advertising are essential to golfing tours and tournaments.

Following page: The 18th hole at Pebble Beach.

rights. It has grown rapidly since then and is now worth over £16 million.

THE SAFARI TOUR

The European PGA Tour is also responsible for organizing the Safari Tour, which is held in the months prior to the Volvo Tour. European golfers get in some competitive practice in Zimbabwe, Nigeria, Kenya, Zambia and the Ivory Coast before the start of the gruelling Volvo Tour.

manufacturer in 1978, is Europe's equivalent of the US PGA Tour.

The Tour as we know it today started in 1971 when former Ryder Cup captain and leading golf teacher, John Jacobs, was appointed by the PGA to organize tournament play for Europe's professionals.

In Jacob's first season prize-money was £250,000 but within four years it had doubled. As the events increased in popularity, the Tournament Players split from the PGA in 1977 and merged with the Continental Tournament Players to form the European Players' Division of the PGA. Prize-money in 1978 exceeded £1 million, thanks largely to television

THE AUSTRALIAN TOUR

Competitive golf is now available all the year round for the leading professional; when it is winter in America or Europe they can make their way to Oceania for the Australian Tour. The New Zealand Open, Australian Open and Australian Masters are prestigious events and many of the top professionals from both sides of the Atlantic make the trip 'Down Under'. The quality of the Australian Tour can be seen in the wealth of talented golfers it has produced in recent years: Greg Norman, David Graham, Ian Baker-Finch, Rodger Davis, Mike Harwood, and many more.

Justin Leonard plays a short iron at the 9th hole of the US PGA, Winged Foot, 1997.

THE PGA SENIORS' TOUR

Held in the United States, the Seniors Tour has grown in popularity in recent years with great players joining such as Jack Nicklaus, Lee Trevino, Gary Player, Arnold Palmer.

Players can join the Seniors' Tour upon reaching the age of 50 and the top money winner can expect to take home far more prize-money than he ever did during his days on the regular Tour. The top money winner in 1991, Mike Hill, won more than $1 million. which was more than Corey Pavin, the top earner on the regular Tour.

Nick Faldo displeased at his shot during the World Match-play Championship in 1992.

THE ASIAN TOUR

One of the fastest growing tours in recent years, the Asian Tour started as the Far East Tour back in 1959 with the first Hong Kong Open. But since then the golf boom has exploded beyond all expectations in Asia, particularly in Japan.

In recent years, top American and European golfers have competed in Japan which has helped boost the popularity of the Asian Tour, not to mention its prize-money, making it one of the richest tours.

THE SUNSHINE TOUR

South Africa, like Australia, offers European and American golfers the chance of winter golf, courtesy of the Sunshine Tour. Many of today's top South African golfers, such as 1992 and 1994 US PGA champion Nick Price, started their professional careers on this tour.

American Meg Mallon won her first two Majors, the US Open and the LPGA in 1991.

Below: Laura Davies (right) with Alison Nicholas after their 1992 Solheim Cup success. Davies was the first British golfer to make a break-through on the US Women's Tour when she won the US Open in 1987.

THE WOMEN'S TOURS

THE US LPGA TOUR

The US LPGA Tour is continuing to grow, and in 1992 total purses were nearly $21 million, with the top money winner each year expecting to take home somewhere in the region of $3/4 million.

It has come a long way since its early years after the formation of the Ladies' Professional Golf Association (LPGA) in 1944. But, thanks largely to financial support from Wilson, the sports manufacturer, the Tour started to gain in popularity and within two years the number of events had grown from 7 to 21. The Tour was on the verge of collapsing in the 1970s after it expanded too quickly, but was saved and its first Commissioner, Ray Volpe, was appointed. He took the Tour into the 1980s with its future looking healthy and prosperous again. Television coverage aided its growth and in the early 1990s it included 40 events.

THE WOMENS' EUROPEAN TOUR

The Womens' European Tour doesn't enjoy the fortune of the US LPGA Tour, largely due to the lack of television coverage, which means reduced sponsorship and smaller prizes. In the early 1990s the number of events was a little over a quarter of its American counterpart. Nevertheless, the European Tour has been responsible for producing one of the world's top women golfers in recent years, Laura Davies.

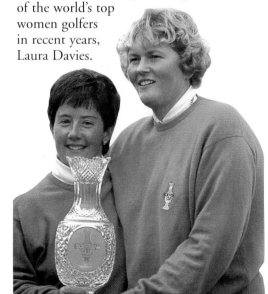

GREAT GOLF COURSES

With golf's increasing popularity,
the number of courses is growing
all the time. The courses included
in this chapter have all hosted the
major tournaments, been the scene
for triumphs and disappointments,
and provided challenges to the
great golfers.

BRITISH ISLES

THE BELFRY

Since its opening in 1977 the Belfry, near Sutton Coldfield in the West Midlands, has rapidly risen to the fore of British golf and is now one of its senior venues, as well as being the home of the PGA.

It was designed by Dave Thomas and Peter Alliss and has very close similarities to the Augusta National Course in America, with water a plentiful feature.

Thomas and Alliss developed two courses, the Derby Course and the championship Brabazon Course. And it was over the latter that British golf has witnessed sone of its greatest scenes. In 1985, Tony Jacklin and his team wrested the Ryder Cup from the Americans after their 28-year dominance. Four years later (after winning in 1987 at Muirfield Village, Ohio) the European team retained the trophy after a nail-biting draw, only to lose it again at The Belfry in 1993.

Apart from hosting the Ryder Cup since 1985, it is the home of the English Open each year. It has also played host to the State Express Classic and Lawrence Batley Classic.

Right: The beauty of the Belfry is captured in this picture of the 10th hole.

Opposite: Valderrama.

ROYAL BIRKDALE

One of many links courses on the Fylde coast of England, situated between Liverpool and Blackpool, Royal-Birkdale is the best known.

The club was founded in 1889 but was situated nearer to Southport town centre than the existing course. They moved to their present site in 1897 and the clubhouse now stands proudly as one of the finest in England.

Birkdale received its 'Royal' status in 1951 and three years later staged its first British Open which was won by Australia's Peter Thomson. America's Arnold Palmer won the next championship to be held there in 1961. On his way to victory he played one of golf's great shots when he hit the ball from behind a bush to within 15 feet of the pin, 140 yards away at the 15th.

Thomson won his fifth post-war Open over the Southport links in 1965. Lee Trevino was Open champion at Birkdale in 1971 and in 1976 the potential of Spanish youngster Severiano Ballesteros was witnessed when he finished second to winner Johnny Miller.

Tom Watson, like Thomson, won his fifth Open at Birkdale, in 1983, and the 1991 Open champion at the famous links was Australia's Ian Baker-Finch.

The large crowd at Royal Birkdale watching Ian Baker-Finch win in 1991.

Lytham, the most northerly English course to stage the British Open.

ROYAL LYTHAM

The Royal Lytham and St Anne's links was originally laid out in 1886 and in 1893 hosted its first championship, the British Ladies' Championship.

The club moved a short distance up the road to its present site on the Fylde Coast close to Blackpool in 1896 and in 1926 was granted 'Royal' status. That same year it hosted its first British Open, which was won by the great amateur Bobby Jones.

When the Open was next held at Lytham, 26 years later, the champion was South Africa's Bobby Locke; and his great

Play the XL CHALLENGER
The famous Half-crown Ball for half the price

OPEN GOLF CHAMPIONSHIP
ROYAL LYTHAM and ST ANNE'S—1926

ORDER OF PLAY
Price - - 6d.

GOLF MONTHLY
The Greatest Golf Paper
Always magnificently illustrated, the Leading Golfers write for it, and it gives the most Exclusive News

rival of the day, Peter Thomson, won in 1958. While it is a flat course, the wind that blows in from the sea makes Lytham as testing as any seaside course and accuracy off the tee is essential. One man who mastered the course, was Tony Jacklin who became the first home winner of the British Open for 18 years in 1969.

Surprisingly, Tom Lehman in 1996, was the first American professional winner of the Open at Royal Lytham. Apart from those mentioned, New Zealander Bob Charles won in 1963, South Africa's Gary Player in 1974, and Spain's Seve Ballesteros twice in 1979 and 1988.

The dog-leg 4th hole at Wentworth.

the Ryder Cup which was inaugurated a year later.

The other major event played at Wentworth was the Canada Cup (now the World Cup) in 1956 when Hogan and Snead captured the title, while Player won the individual title. It is now the home of the Volvo PGA Championship, one of the leading events on the annual Volvo Tour.

WENTWORTH

As it is not a links course, Wentworth is not eligible to host the British Open. Nevertheless, it is still one of England's best-known courses,and has been used for the World Match-play Championship every year since its inauguration in 1964. It also hosted the Ryder Cup in 1953.

Located close to London at Virginia Water in Surrey, the original East course was opened in 1924 and the West course followed in the 1930s. At nearly 7,000 yards in length, the latter eventually became the championship course, and because of its length earned the nickname 'The Burma Road'. The par 5 17th is the longest hole at 571 yards, But to make the closing holes challenging, the 18th is also a par 5 and measures more than 500 yards.

Shortly after Wentworth opened, it hosted a challenge match between the professionals of Great Britain and the United States. This was the forerunner of

CARNOUSTIE

The longest course ever to stage the British Open, Carnoustie measured 7,272 yards when it hosted its fourth Open in 1968. Even the champion, Gary Player, could not bring the giant to its knees - his winning total of 289 was the highest for 21 years. Built at Angus in Scotland in 1842, the natural terrain and hazards ensure that the closing three holes are probably the toughest in Britain.

Above: the 18th at Carnoustie.

The famous Gleneagles Hotel.

The brook, called the Barry Burn, which weaves its way across the course, comes into play at five holes and three times at the 18th.

America's Tommy Armour won Carnoustie's first Open in 1931, and in 1937 Henry Cotton won his second Open there. When Ben Hogan won in 1953 he certainly tamed the giant course. Tom Watson won his first title at Carnoustie in 1975.

GLENEAGLES

Situated at Auchterarder in Perthshire, and surrounded by the Ochils and Grampian mountains, it has one of the most beautiful settings in British Golf. The Kings and Queens courses opened in 1919 and the Gleneagles Hotel five years later. The two original courses were designed by James Braid. There are now a total of four courses, all are needed to meet the demands of local and visiting golfers.

The first major individual championship held at Gleneagles was the 1935 Penfold Tournament won by Peter Allis' father, Percy. Because it is not a true links course, Gleneagles has never played host to the British Open, but its survival has not depended on hosting major championships as its beauty has ensured that it is one of the world's most visited golf courses.

MUIRFIELD

Muirfield first hosted the British Open in 1892 when the title was won by Englishman Harold Hilton. One hundred years later, the British Open was played over the famous Scottish course again, and another Englishman, Nick Faldo, carried off the title. It was the fourteenth time that Muirfield, the home of the Honourable Company of Edinburgh Golfers, has hosted the Open. The original layout was designed by Old Tom Morris. Situated on the Firth of Forth, the winds can make conditions extremely hazardous. Severe rough is also a problem at Muirfield but these difficult conditions have provided the setting for some of the most exciting championships. Henry Cotton gave a wonderful display of driving to win the 1948 Open at Muirfield, and in 1966 Jack Nicklaus won his first Open here. In 1971 Lee Trevino deprived

An undated painting of St Andrews.

another Briton, Tony Jacklin of victory, when he chipped in at the 71st for victory.

Because of its location, Muirfield is a perfect course for the spectator and it is for this reason that it has staged most leading tournaments, including the 1973 Ryder Cup when the tournament was played in Scotland for the first time.

ST ANDREWS

The home of golf. The sport has been played in the Burgh of St Andrews since 1552, and possibly earlier.

The Society of St Andrews' Golfers was formed in May 1754 and is one of the world's oldest. In 1834 the Society changed its name to the Royal and Ancient after William IV agreed to become the club's first patron. Twenty years later, and 100 years after the Society's formation, the current clubhouse was built.

By the end of the nineteenth century, the Royal and Ancient was highly respected by other clubs and it became regarded as the authority on the rules of golf. The club still holds this position today.

Situated alongside St Andrews Bay, the original course contains 22 holes but with only 11 greens. Those large, double-holed greens remain a major feature of the Old Course at St Andrews. The 17th, known as the Road Hole, is notorious for being one of the world's most difficult holes. It

Left: The Hell bunker at St Andrews is one of the world's most famous bunkers.

Opposite: The 4th green at Turnberry with the beautiful backdrop of Ailsa Craig.

has claimed many victims over the years as championship-winning rounds have come unstuck at this infamous par 4. A second course, the New Course was constructed in 1894 and before the end of the century, the Jubilee course was completed. A fourth, the Eden course, was added in 1912. St Andrews has hosted over 20 Opens, since its first in 1873, most recently in 1995 when it was the scene of American John Daly's victory after a four hole play-off against Constantino Rocca of Italy.

TURNBERRY

Turnberry had to wait a long time before staging its first British Open, but when it came, in 1977, Tom Watson and Jack

Nicklaus shattered record after record before Watson ran out the one-stroke winner. It staged another Open in 1986, when Australia's Greg Norman was champion, and again in 1994 when Nick Price of South Africa won the tournament.

The backdrop of Ailsa Craig and Isle of Arran offers one of the finest settings in British golf, and has done since the Marquis of Ailsa laid out the first course on his private Scottish estate in the nineteenth century. The Turnberry Hotel Golf Club was established in 1903 and between the two world wars a second course was built, thus providing the Ailsa and Arran courses, the Ailsa is the championship course used today.

The course suffered extensive damage during World War II when it was seconded by the RAF Coastal Command, but was restored to its former glory by 1951. When it staged the News of the World Match-play Championship in 1957 it was hailed as a great championship course by the professionals of the day.

UNITED STATES

AUGUSTA

The Augusta National golf course offers tough demanding golf, and its setting must rank as the finest in the world.

Former champion Bobby Jones had a vision to design the most beautiful course in the world, fit for one of the most prestigious championships in the world - the Masters. He recruited the services of top designer Alister Mackenzie and in 1931 the Augusta course in Georgia was opened. The plant-life is spectacular and the holes are named after the shrubs that line each fairway. Tall pine trees and the abundance of water make Augusta even more attractive, and demanding - the lake in front of the 16th green has seen many ambitions destroyed.

The picturesque 16th hole at Augusta.

The greens also offer a demanding test. The 11th, 12th and 13th holes, known as 'Amen Corner', are alongside Rae's Creek which awaits any wayward shots - something that no player can afford at Augusta.

CYPRESS POINT

While Cypress Point has never been used for a major championship, because it is only 6,506 yards long and not severe enough, it is still one of the top American courses.

Located on the Monterey Peninsula, Cypress Point is very beautiful and its lack of yards does not detract from its severity. The 16th demands the best of tee shots to the green 233 yards away because there is no fairway, just a drop into the Pacific Ocean and the rugged rocks below.

The 1921 US Women's Open Champion Marion Hollins was responsible for Cypress Point after falling in love with California, and with the help of Alister Mackenzie and money donated by local businessmen her course was opened in 1928.

MERION

The Merion Golf Club was founded at Ardmore, Pennsylvania, in 1865. The first golf course of nine holes was laid out at nearby Haverford in 1896. It was extended to 18 holes in 1900, but it was not long enough and the East course at Ardmore was opened in 1912. A second course was added two years later. It has now staged more US Golf Association tournaments than any other American course. While the East course is only 6,468 yards long, with the 2nd and 4th holes both par 5s, Merion offers as tough a start to a round of golf as any course in America.

Merion first hosted the US Open in 1934 when Olin Dutra came from eight behind after 36 holes to take the title, and it was at Merion in 1930 that Bobby Jones completed golf's greatest Grand Slam when he took the US Amateur title.

MUIRFIELD VILLAGE

Designed by Jack Nicklaus, Muirfield Village is named after the Scottish course that was the scene of Nicklaus' first British Open success in 1966.

Although he has helped many other courses world-wide, Nicklaus had the idea of building his own course in his home town of Columbus, Ohio, shortly after winning the 1966 Masters. When he won the British Open a couple of months later, the course found its name.

Knowing what a club and professional player alike wanted out of a golf course, Nicklaus, came up with a course that can be both tough and fair. He also took into consideration the needs of golf fans. Muirfield Village is a good spectator course, which is one reason why it was chosen for the 1987 Ryder Cup - when in fact the Americans lost on home soil for the first time.

Muirfield Village opened in 1976 and since then has played host each year to the Memorial Tournament, one of the US Tour events. Jack Nicklaus has won the title twice.

Left: The 16th tee at Cypress Point.

Previous page: The 16th hole at Cypress Point.

PEBBLE BEACH

Another course on the Monterey Peninsula, opened in 1919, Pebble Beach offers the same scenic grandeur as Cypress Point and it must rank as one of the most spectacular courses in the United States. The 107-yard, par 3 7th at Pebble Beach is probably the most photographed hole in the world as the green juts out into the Pacific.

The 8th is just as spectacular with your second shot requiring a carry over a 100-foot drop into the Pacific, and the par 5 18th, along the rugged coastline, is one of the toughest closing holes in golf. Most golfers are grateful to make par to complete their round. One man who bettered this at the 18th, and also the tough 17th, was Tom Watson on his way to winning the 1982 US Open when he made two birdies to snatch the title from Jack Nicklaus. The course staged two other Opens, in 1972 and 1992.

Below: Sand, sand, everywhere. The view of the par 4 2nd at Pine Valley.

PINE VALLEY

The Pine Valley course was the vision of George Crump. owner of the Colonnades Hotel in Philadelphia, Pennsylvania. Crump wanted to build the best and most demanding golf course in the world. He called in British designer, H.S.Colt, who developed a 184-acre forest area at Clementon, New Jersey, in order to fulfil Crump's dream.

The course was opened in 1916 and three years later its 14 holes were extended to 18. Crump's dream of making it one of the best and toughest courses in the world was realized, and it immediately gained respect from professional golfers of the day. The countless bunkers add to Pine Valley's severity. The 367-yard, par 4 2nd hole presents one of the most daunting tasks in golf as you stand on the tee and see little else but bunkers along the fairway.

Above and right: After the difficult short 7th, the 8th at Pebble Beach offers no respite.

SHINNECOCK HILLS

Shinnecock Hills is named after the tribe Shinnecock Indians who used to live in South-eastern Long Island where the course is located. The club was formed in 1891 by businessman Wiliam Vanderbilt and is one of the oldest still-surviving clubs in America. America's first 18-hole course opened in 1891 and a year later, the magnificent clubhouse, designed by Stanford White, was inaugurated. The course was designed by the club's first professional, Willie Dunn, and reflects many features of the courses in his Scottish homeland.

Shinnecock Hills played host to the second US Open in 1896 but did not host its second championship until 1986 when Ray Floyd became the oldest champion at the age of 43.

The course was regarded as too short for the professionals of the 1930s and it was unlikely to be regarded as a championship course again unless it was extended. So in the 1930s Dick Wilson was called in to make major changes. It now measures 6,740 yards.

EUROPE

VALDERRAMA (SPAIN)

Spain's Costa Del Sol has gained a reputation for being one of the foremost golfing centres in Europe in the last decade and Valderrama boasts one of Spain's finest, if not oldest, golf clubs. It is often referred to as 'Europe's Augusta'.

Valderrama was laid out in the picturesque Sotogrande area of Spain in 1964 and within two years it was hosting the Spanish Open, which Argentina's Roberto de Vincenzo won.

The course was revamped in the 1980s and turned into a course testing enough to meet the demands of the golf professional. Its closing nine holes now provide one of the toughest tests on the European Tour. In 1997, Valderrama was the first golf course outside Britain to stage the Ryder Cup, which was memorable for the nerve-wracking European victory.

ST NOM-LA-BRÊTECHE (FRANCE)

The home of one of the Volvo Tour's top events, the Lâncome Trophy, since its launch in 1970, the St Nom-la-Brêteche course is situated close to Versailles.

The original course was designed by British designer Fred Hawtree. A second course was added later and there are now two courses; the Red and the Blue. It has

The closing hole at Valderrama, described as 'Spain's Augusta'.

been used to host many domestic championships including the French Open on three occasions, the third time being in 1982 when Spain's Severiano Ballesteros won the title. The first winner in 1965 was Seve's uncle Ramon Sota. The other French Open held at St Nom-la-Brêteche, in 1969, was won by Jean Garaialde who became the first Frenchman for 22 years to win his home Open.

PENINA (PORTUGAL)

Think of Penina and you think of one man: Henry Cotton. It was after retiring in 1964 that the three-times British Open champion developed the Penina golf course in the Algarve area of Portugal.

The climate makes Penina a popular venue with tourists and aspiring professionals and each autumn the PGA takes young hopefuls to Penina to carry on the tradition started by Cotton, who died in 1987.

The inward nine holes at Penina offer some of the toughest golf in Europe and the last nine holes start and finish with two par 5s, thus making the inward par of 38 a difficult target. But Cotton's course is as fair as it is tough, and pre-planning at every hole is important. The foolhardy will find themselves paying for their mistakes.

The 9th at Penina.

Above: Action from the 1989 European Masters-Swiss Open at Crans-sur-Sierre.

CRANS-SUR-SIERRE (SWITZERLAND)

For a spectacular setting, Switzerland's Crans-sur-Sierre course, with the backdrop of the Matterhorn, takes some beating.

Situated 5,000 feet above the Rhône Valley, the original course was laid out by skiing holiday pioneer Sir Arnold Lunn in 1905 after he had already built the nearby Palace Hotel. In 1927 the current course was opened and golf in the area has grown in popularity since then.

The Swiss Open has been played at Crans since 1939 and it was during the 1961 Open that Italy's Baldovino Dassu shot a European Tour 18-hole record 60. And in the 1978 Open Spain's José-Maria Olazabal shot a European Tour 9-hole record 27. It is the largest club in Switzerland but the snow-covered fairways necessitate its closure in the winter months.

AROUND THE WORLD

The 6th hole at Royal Melbourne.

ROYAL MELBOURNE (AUSTRALIA)

Royal Melbourne offers the golfer a mixture of Augusta's beauty, and the characteristics of many of the Scottish links courses. It is one of the great championship courses outside Britain and America.

The first course was laid out in 1891 and has had constant membership since that date. The course moved from its original site to the Sandringham area of Melbourne in 1901 and in the 1920s Alister Mackenzie was called in to redesign it.

A second course, the East course, was added in 1932 and such is the design of the two that holes from both can be incorporated into one 18-hole championship course as and when needed.

The greens are very fast because they are relaid every five or six years, and at the 6th and 14th holes the amateur and professional alike is faced with the testing dog-legs which both require correct club selection, followed by an accurate drive. Royal Melbourne hosted the World Cup in 1959 when Peter Thomson and Kel Nagle provided home winners. When it was played at Royal Melbourne again in 1972 Taiwan were the surprise victors.

251

ROYAL CALCUTTA (INDIA)

Formed in 1829, the Royal Calcutta
Club is the oldest club outside Britain,
and the Indian Amateur Championship,
which has been held at the course since
1892, is one of the oldest championships
in the world. The club received 'Royal'
patronage from King George V in 1911.

The original course was laid out in the
Dum Dum area of Calcutta, where
Calcutta's international airport is now
situated. The club moved to the
Tollygunge area of Calcutta and over the
years the site, which was once a paddy-
field, has been developed into one of the
great golf courses of the world.

To the uninitiated, the course looks
easy; but it is not. The par 4s are decep-
tive, and require good iron play off the
fairways, and the small greens are filled
with hidden rolls and undulations.

GLEN ABBEY (CANADA)

The home of the Royal Canadian Golf
Association, Glen Abbey was one of the
first purpose-built golf courses to meet
the excessive demands of golf in the
boom years of the 1970s.

Jack Nicklaus was asked to assist with
the design and he took full advantage of
the natural features of the area close to
Lake Ontario in the Oakville district of
Ontario.

*Jack Nicklaus, who assisted in the design of
Glen Abbey.*

As with his own Muirfield Village course,
Nicklaus gave consideration to the spectator as well as providing a tough test for
the golfer.

Nicklaus did not have to start from
scratch, because a course had been laid
out in the 1960s, but his task was a major
re-building. With the exception of 1980,
Glen Abbey has been the permanent
home of the Canadian Open since 1977,
the year after it opened.

INDEX